THE UNDERHANDED SERVE

OR HOW TO PLAY DIRTY TENNIS

THE UNDERHANDED SERVE
OR HOW TO PLAY DIRTY TENNIS

by REX LARDNER

Illustrated by Arthur Wallower

Hawthorn Books, Inc., Publishers

New York

THE UNDERHANDED SERVE

Library of Congress Catalog Card Number: 68-30708
ISBN: 0-8015-8142-7

Design: Gene Gordon

6   7   8   9   10

Hawthorn Books, Inc., gratefully acknowledges permission to reprint material that first appeared in the following publications: *The New York Times,* copyright © 1965, 1966, by The New York Times Company; *Cavalier* magazine; *World Tennis* magazine, reprinted by permission of *World Tennis* and its editor and publisher, Gladys M. Heldman.

Contents

Introduction

If you know anything about sports you know that tennis is a game of controlled speed. The emphasis is on control. If speed is all that's important, why is not George Gustafson (mentioned in Chapter 3) champion of the world? Provided, of course, he can work himself into some kind of shape.

The factor of control makes tennis a unique game physically and psychologically. There are at least eleven elements involved in making even a *bad* forehand drive and more for a bad backhand. Hitting a proper shot is much more complex. The winning player is the one who can maintain physical and mental control in spite of the efforts of the opposing side—and in some cases the unwitting actions of his own partner—to throw him off.

Tennis is not a game of physical contact (unless you are afflicted, as I have been, with an overzealous doubles partner), but in no sport does psychology play a more vital role. That is why so many psychiatrists play—though I have found they are among the first to blow up. Your opponent, by one means and another, is trying to make you lose concentration, confidence, and equanimity; if you are any kind of competitor you are doing the same with him. It is either that or kill him.

But there are rewards. In the middle of a hard-fought set, seeing your opponent hurl his racket at the fence after a bad shot or use his best serve to loft the ball far over the fence is sweeter than wine.

This book takes up most of the psychological gambits I have observed and been tested by over the years, indoors and out, winter and summer, in "friendly" matches and tournaments, along with countergambits and other advice the competitive player may find useful. If he does not—tough.

1

Scorer's Advantage

For some obscure historical or etymological reason I am not going to go into, scoring in tennis is not one, two, three, four as in every other racket game and all varieties of handball (to say nothing of soccer and polo), but is a fancy "15–30–40–game." There is the additional complication of 40–40 being called "deuce." After that you go to somebody's advantage and maybe back to deuce and somebody else's advantage and maybe *then* to game. A lot of people have turned to squash and golf because of this, and God knows how many Davis Cup possibilities we have lost because some young man could not master the complexities of the system.

On the other hand, the mysterious origins of the scoring and the size of the numbers (in football a touchdown is only 6) give rise to a lot of intellectual debate (Is 30–all the same as deuce? Can you have advantage out in the backhand court? Which is the backhand court for a left-hander?) and lend the function of keeping score more importance than that of almost any other sport. For instance, in baseball, a runner either crosses the plate safely or he does not; after an argument and a decision the run counts or it does not. But in tennis, after an argument whether a ball was either in or out and one side conceding, figuring he or they will get it back within the next few points, you have to have a discussion about the score. What does that make it? the concedee will ask, and a new argument starts as the conceding party tries to win the point back by verbal methods.

(I am referring, naturally, to matches played without benefit of an umpire—early rounds in small tournaments and so-called friendly matches played at clubs and on rich men's courts and public courts. An umpire, when there is one, keeps track of the score for all the players in a particular match and announces it after every point, game, and set. Furthermore, if he has any brains, he writes it down so there can be no argument on the part of one player that it is the fourth set when it is really the fifth, and so on. Any upsetting of the opposite side has to be done by methods other than the way scorekeeping is handled.)

It is my feeling that of all the psychological devices used to upset an opponent in tennis (and most of them have been practiced on me), the most devastating is the way the score is kept—the way it is announced, how much despair it engenders, and how much heat is fanned up when it is argued about. You can intimidate an opponent, disrupt his equanimity, destroy his confidence, shatter his nerves, and make him fly into a blind rage by the way you keep score. Or, in some cases, *fail* to keep it. Let me illustrate.

At a club where I used to belong I was badly beating Sam ——. I had won the first two sets 6–0, 6–0, but because I know that some players do not like to have the score announced after every point or game (especially when they are taking a shellacking like I was giving Sam), I called it out only occasionally. Sam hardly spoke at all. After I won the first five games of the third set, I mentioned that the score was 5–0. "It's one–love," Sam insisted absently. "It's at least three–love," I said, annoyed at his lapse of memory. (This is the trouble with not allowing your opponent to win any games; he is only interested in his zero, and the games you pile up do not register on his consciousness.)

"Don't you remember my saying it was two–love about ten minutes ago? I asked. "That was the first set," he murmured. "This is the second set." I digested the remark with a little difficulty. Somewhere, in the midst of all the rallying, feelings of triumph and frustration, cries of "Out!" and "Double fault!", an entire set had vanished.

"Compromise at two–love," I said, resigned to the fact that I was pitted against an amnesiac. We settled on 2–0 and I was so disturbed by having a set and three games taken away from me that I won the set only 6–4. Furthermore, I am sure that Sam, judging by the smug expression he wore as we walked off the court and the jolly way he waved to friends, was under the impression he had won it, 8–6. I have not played him since.

There are other problems. The fact that "thirty" sounds like "forty" and vice versa when the score is shouted across the net often causes confusion that breaks your concentration and drives you into a rage. The server and receiver will stand directly opposite one another instead of diagonally opposite, and the server will say: "You're in the wrong court." "What's the score?" the receiver will ask. "Forty–fifteen." "It can't be thirty–fifteen." "I said *forty*–fifteen." "Not in this court." "*You're in the wrong court!*" And so on.

A friend of mine who was in the Navy solves this difficulty by saying, "Thirty (three-oh) playing fifteen" and "Forty (four-oh) playing thirty (three-oh)," whenever the situations arise. So when I play him I sometimes announce: "Fifteen (one-five) mark zero zero. Down 'scope . . . Fire one! Fire two!" Which, I regret to say, he often finds quite disconcerting.

The women on the next court can drive you crazy with their discussion of the score, especially if it is doubles. "Is that forty–thirty or thirty–forty?" one of them will start, leading to a convention at the net. "Oh, it must be

Scoring Problem

thirty–fifteen, because I only received once." "Don't you remember? You're not receiving. Your side is serving." "Then it must be thirty–love." "No, it's thirty–forty, because I remember thinking if we won the next point it would be game." "I know Phyllis missed one shot completely." "If she's serving in the ad court it must be deuce." "I thought I just served there." "Then it must be somebody's ad." "Who won the first point?" "Why don't we call it deuce? I love your hair, Phyllis." "That wouldn't be right if it's really forty–thirty." "But what if it's thirty–forty?" "I know Phyllis hit one shot into the net." "Could it be fifteen–all?" "Not if she's serving in this court." "But she just served there!" "Why don't we call it love–fifteen?" And so on.

One trouble with getting the score wrong is that it affects the tactics you use—whether you are going to make sure that you return every shot or whether you are going to go crazy and run up to the net. A player with 40–0 against him cannot risk aiming for the lines, whereas if he leads by that amount he can lose two points in spectacular ways (especially if there is an audience) before he really has to worry.

The score also affects the amount of courtesy you are going to show to an opponent. If you are ahead 5–1 and 40–15 and your opponent serves a ball that comes close to the line that you hit back and then call out, you may be tempted—after he favors you with a long look—to let him have two serves instead of the official and legal single serve he has remaining. But if *he* is winning by this score and a similar exchange occurs, you are constrained to abide by the official, legal rules, and he has only one more chance to get the ball in the proper service box. "One fault coming!" is how I give him the news.

It is the same with an out shot that your opponent, charging up to the net, wildly claims was in. If you are behind, you insist on calling shots on your side of the net; but if you are comfortably ahead—about 5–0, 30–0, say

—you can morally allow the replay of the point. This kind of courtesy pays off in the long run.

Some players put pressure on you by being totally unable to keep track of the score from point to point and are constantly badgering you to reveal it. They act surprised when you start banging balls at them and tell them the game is over. Then, of course, they are curious about the game score. Some want to know the game score between points. Sometimes you tell a player the score without his asking for it and this reminds him that he does not know what the score is. "What does that make it?" he will ask. It is like going to a backwards movie.

Some players, when you hit a shot close to the line, never let you know whether it was in or out. They do not even give you a hint by acting agonized or elated. You cannot ask them whether the shot was good or not because that lets them know you have doubts and that starts the wheels turning in their minds. The only way you can find out is to interrupt their reverie and ask them what the score is. Of course, you have to make sure they do not give it to you reversed—15–30 for 30–15, for instance—because this can cause you great befuddlement later on. So you have to stand in the middle of the net, get your opponent's attention, and say, "Your fifteen, my thirty. Right?" And you assume the shot must have been good. Then your opponent will reply, "No. My thirty, your fifteen." Now you know the shot was out.

Some players in doubles will announce the score wrong, and when you correct them they start hollering the right score as if someone else had volunteered the incorrect one and they are now clearing up all doubts. One gentleman I play knows what a purist I am about keeping the correct score, so just before he serves to me in doubles he announces the score wrong. "Thirty–fifteen," he will say when it is really love–40. I have to shout the correct score at him and justify it. This procedure always costs me the next point. Then, "Our ad," he will say. "No! *Our* ad!" I will call to him. It is almost always immediately deuce. I played one opponent (no longer) who called out the word "foot" when you hit twelve inches or so beyond the baseline. This sounds so much like "Good!" that some terrific misunderstandings ensued until his idiosyncrasy was revealed. If there is a high wind blowing against me, I am in bad trouble because I have to shout across the net and the length of the court several times a game. This is tough on your vocal chords, to say nothing of your temper.

A few players I know who can at least keep track of the score annoy you in other ways. They have peculiar ways of saying "Deuce"—like "dyooss" or "dooz"—that can throw you off your game. A player I know says "Murad" (the name of an old cigarette) for "Your ad." It is worth about four points a set to him when he plays me. Some players imitate the sonorous singsong of umpires at Forest Hills—"Fiyuff-teen . . . For-ty"—to show they are world-class players, which is very irritating. A characteristic of many players I know is that they announce the score only when they are so far ahead in points that you have very little chance to catch up, their vocabulary being limited to 40–love and love–40. If you are ahead, they prefer to pretend no score is being kept. Some players make you lose concentration by saying "Forty–all" for deuce. Some players put pressure on you, when the situation arises, by saying "Point set" (that provoking phrase) or "Set point." *Their* set point, naturally. Even worse is "triple set point," which subtly informs you that you have to capture three straight points just to reach deuce. When it is my triple set point I do not make use of this phrase but merely ask my opponent what the score is and stare at him thoughtfully for seven seconds to make sure he knows what calamity will ensue should he lose any one of the next three points. I once heard the phrase "point point set," which means the set can be won if a particular player wins two successive points. I resolved, if I ever played this gentleman, that after the first point of the first game I would say, "Fifteen–love. Point point point point point point point point . . . set." But the opportunity never arose.

Still another way the score can affect the outcome of a match is when you pause to have an intellectual discussion about it. One time in an important match at another club I used to belong to, I was running my opponent all over the court and after a rally I mentioned that the score was deuce. "It's thirty–all," he corrected me. "It's the same thing," I said quietly. We had a relatively calm discussion about it, during which time he managed to recover his breath. I won the argument, and he won the match. Sometimes you can be too knowledgeable for your own good.

2

The Valiant Outdoorsmen

In the past few years there has been, as I probably do not need to point out, a tremendous boom in indoor tennis, with courts sprouting up all over the place—some carved out of city buildings, railroad depots, and factories; others, in the suburbs, enclosed by inflated balloons and edifices of wood, stucco, St. Joseph's brick, fiberglass, random range, and steel. They are all partly supported by plenty of overhead girders, joists, beams, slabs, and purlins, making the lob an interesting shot. They are lit by everything from carbon lamps to bluish fluorescent tubes you could hold a séance by or giant klieg spots that encourage a return to the underhand serve. If some of them contain shadowy backcourt areas where the ball enters a different time continuum for a split second, that makes you get up to net where doubles should be played anyway. The courts are reserved so you do not have the aggravation of trying to chase other players off after they have breezed through several leisurely sets. If the season rate is divided up among four or five people (including the price of tennis balls), it costs no more than running a yacht. Probably the biggest kick comes from being able to play under Hawaiian-type conditions when the weather is bad outside or playing at night when the rest of the world is watching *The Late Late Show.*

Personally, I am not much for indoor tennis. The reasons I will take up shortly, but mainly it is because I am used to, and see no reason for abandoning, tennis outdoors in the winter. When this season comes, with its howling gales, blankets of snow, and erratic blasts of bone-chilling wind, some sturdy friends of mine and I— along with other dedicated residents of northern Long Island—play our most competitive tennis. Naturally, a lot of preparations are necessary. For instance, from November on, I am never without a long-handled broom in my car. Or a couple of stiff whisk brooms for extra-fine work. Albert Grundy, another member of the group, has the back of his station wagon full of old rags. Joe Gruler, another member, owns the largest, heaviest snow shovel ever built. The handle alone weighs fifteen pounds, but it intimidates lightweight snow. (If you catch the snow as it falls, or right afterward, you can clear half a tennis court in twenty minutes.) Gordon Briggs carries around a tennis net in the back seat of his Jeep, and Don Klaver has in the trunk of his Edsel boxes of red and yellow tennis balls —easier to distinguish against a snowy background and a dull gray sky. Esmond Lafferty furnishes ice picks and a trowel.

Other Long Islanders are similarly equipped, all of them members of an intrepid band of athletes who have given up other winter sports, including tennis indoors, for this most challenging of games. While some of our contemporaries are comfortably hitting lobs into girders, we don mufflers, sheepskin coats, earmuffs, sweat suits, ski masks, Tibetan climbing hats, and special gloves for the adventure. (The gloves, made of chamois with a terry-cloth backing, were originally used by players prone to developing blisters or a slithery palm in summer heat. Then Outdoorsmen, as we are called, found that the gloves

When Wintry Winds Blow

are ideal for warmth without sacrificing racket feel and adopted them for winter play.)

Thus colorfully protected against the elements, we proceed to unbury, as it were, a nearby cement or asphalt court. My broom is used to sweep off the snow that Gruler has missed, especially on the lines, or to thin out puddles formed by melted snow or ice. The trowels and ice picks are used to chip away ice that has stayed solid. Grundy's rags are to blot large puddles. Sometimes he ties them to his galoshes and does a clog dance in the water. Briggs's net is used when the local courts are filled up with Outdoorsmen, and we have to travel to a court that may not be equipped with a net in winter. It takes only about fifteen minutes to string it up. Playing without a net changes the whole complexion of the game and none of us will do it.

Curiously, we were not always outdoor tennis players. Somewhat hopefully, when past autumn equinoxes rolled around, we took up such cold-weather pursuits as skiing, skating, squash, platform tennis, and paddle tennis. And, briefly, tennis indoors. Finally we hit on the Outdoorsmen's game as the most aesthetically satisfying winter sport.

Skiing is not much fun because you have those big, heavy slats on your feet that impede movement. And there are no *tactics* involved—no feints or tricky maneuvers or arguing about the score to let your doubles partner catch his breath. These are what lend spice to tennis, no matter what the season.

In skating, your feet freeze, and some nut is always cutting across in front of you as though it were the Olympics.

Squash is fine for some. You play dressed in shorts in a tiny room a little bit colder than Novaya Zemlya—most often with a maniac who will stop at nothing to get to and swat the ball. For a couple of months a few years ago, I was stoic about getting hit in the back of the head with the ball and whacked across the spine with the racket while getting in a few licks of my own. But what finished me as a squash enthusiast was hitting a hard serve that my opponent missed completely, turning to gloat, and getting socked in the eye with the ball when my opponent whirled around and took it off the back wall. I conceded him the game and my equipment then and there.

Neither platform tennis nor paddle tennis, both of which are played outdoors, is very satisfactory for the avid tennis player. The rules are funny, the courts are too small to allow sweep to your drives, you can get killed while playing net, and the racket, having no strings, feels like a log in your hands when you hit.

I have mentioned some of the advantages of indoor tennis, which seems to have an appeal for a great many players. However, for me the game was, and still is, an unmitigated disaster. The first time I played, the court looked eight feet too long; when I complained to the pro, he told me it was a matter of perspective. This information did not help. My best serves plunked into the middle of the net. Whatever lobs got through the mass of girders, joists, and purlins overhead fell short and got smashed.

I worked out a scientific explanation for the phenomenon: Because there is no place for the air to escape, when you hit a ball indoors the air piles up in front of it, molecules and atoms clustering together to form a force shield impeding its progress. The pro said this theory was nonsense—that the reason I hit short was psychological, that I was being intimidated by the ceiling overhead and the surrounding walls. Dollar signs floating before his eyes, he said I would get used to it, but I never did.

Still another objection was the hour or two-hour time limit and the precision with which it was enforced. None of our group relished the way the foursome that had engaged the court for the session following ours would appear fifteen minutes early, stand around like ghosts, and then, when the wall clock hand clicked, intercept the ball in the middle of a rally, say Thank you for being so punctual, and commandeer the court.

On the few occasions I have played indoors lately, special rules dreamed up by the players have puzzled me. In one group, the receiver is not allowed to hit the ball at the net man on the second serve—presumably because the second serve is so weak that the net man's ribs are in danger. Also, a first serve that hits the net and bounces over but lands outside the service box is taken over just like a let ball—presumably this rule reduces the number of double faults, but it also gives the receiver a legal shot at the net man that he might resent having taken away from him. Once in a nighttime doubles game with a different group I had a perfect opportunity for a drop shot, so I hit a beauty. As one of our opponents lumbered up to it he grumbled, "What are the ground rules on *that?*" So, indoors, apparently, the drop shot has gone the way of the kidney punch. I am waiting for some group to bar the smash.

About two years ago, at a cocktail party at Gruler's house where a bunch of us were lamenting the end of outdoor tennis weather and the mental hazards of the indoor game, Lafferty suggested playing golf in the winter, regardless of the weather. Briggs pointed out that you could never shovel snow off an entire golf course (he had apparently never heard of red golf balls and winter rules), and amid much merriment the suggestion was vetoed. Whereupon Grundy suggested that we play outdoor tennis in the winter, regardless of weather, and, since we were all at the top of our games, we became enthusiastic. We settled on times and places, assigned chores, toasted the plan, and were shortly in business.

There are many advantages to playing outdoor tennis in winter, apart from the fresh air and exercise, the creation of special stratagems, and the challenge of adapting oneself to terrifying conditions. There are, for instance, no lady doubles players taking up the courts and laughing and giggling gaily as they miss a shot just as you are

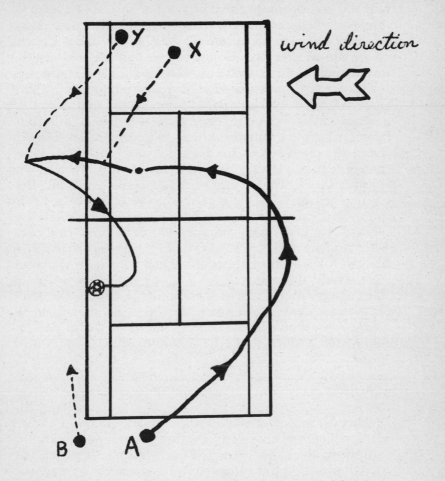

Outdoor Tactics I: With a violent crosswind blowing, Player A hits a lob with underspin. Judging ball's curved flight, Player X runs to position himself for smash. Player Y (author) moves to a point behind X and far out of court, where he can hit ball if X misses it—as he does. Y now smashes into the wind, the ball curving back out of B's reach for a clean placement.

about to serve. If the courts happen to be crowded with male players, nobody plays more than two sets because the players waiting will brain them if they stay on any longer. Nobody feels too bad if he misses a difficult shot because there are so many reasons why you can miss—a shifting crosswind, sleet in your eye, the ball hitting a wet spot on the court, your partner swinging at the ball simultaneously, fear of slipping and breaking a metatarsal.

Because of frequent inclement weather, the strokes used in outdoor winter tennis are somewhat different from the classic ones used by players like Vines, Perry, and Budge when they are on a well-kept dry court and playing under ideal conditions. For instance, rather than hitting the ball flat, your winter player likes to get a lot of strings on the ball—for better control, pace, and accuracy. He also must concentrate more, preparing for a shot a great deal sooner (or later) because of the wind factor. A common practice to determine where and when one should move for the ball is tossing snow in the air between points to assess the wind's speed and direction. While everyone in our group does not hit the ball in the same way (thank God), here are descriptions of some of the strokes adopted by the better outdoor players.

Forehand

This is the most useful shot in the game—for deep drives, paving the way for a volley at net, and hitting lobs into or against the wind. The ball must be watched very closely after your opponent hits it, since it may veer sharply after crossing the net. You take a very short backswing, make ready to jump to either side, and, holding the arm at about a 45-degree angle, swoop down on the ball, drawing the strings across it. If you imagine the ball as a clock, the aim point is about 7:15 P.M. to begin with but you finish at about 2:25. After the ball is struck, the wrist moves down and under to impart extra control. There is no follow-through. The drive is also used to slam the ball into the back fence after a blunder by your partner.

Backhand

In doubles—which is what we are talking about—very little use is made of this shot. But if—because of a treacherous wind shift or because one's partner falls down—it is unavoidable, this is the procedure: Quickly change the grip, bring the feet around so they are perpendicular to the net, lock the right leg in place, fling the left knee back in the manner of a fencer making a lunge, and, with the elbow sharply bent, bring the racket through the ball at about a 65-degree angle. At the conclusion of the stroke the feet should be pointed toward the left sideline and the body moving backward to make ready for your opponent's return.

The Smash

This stroke is hit like the serve.

The Serve

This is the most difficult shot in the game. The ball cannot be tossed high or the wind will carry it several feet one way or the other, and the server may be forced to strike it while rapidly backing up or diving forward, much like a naturalist chasing a butterfly. The toss should never be higher than the head, and there should be very little backswing. The ball is struck at about the height of the right shoulder with a great deal of slice. The first serve is mainly for testing purposes and seldom goes in (indeed, for some players in my group it seldom goes in in summer, either).

When serving against the wind it is wise to aim for the trees behind the court, since the wind will probably pull the ball down. With the wind, the aim point is the middle of the net. If it is raining or hailing and you wear glasses, it is a good idea to let the ball drop lower than the shoulder, so you will not have to look up, and serve side-arm, putting a great deal of overspin on the ball if the wind is behind you, underspin if it is blowing at you, and left-to-right sidespin if a crosswind is blowing. For purposes of deception the same grip is used as for the forehand.

Other strokes—the lob, volley, half-volley, stop volley, drop shot, chop, and slice—are hit in the same way, always making allowances for the speed and direction of the wind, wet spots on the court, and the stupidity of your partner.

I cannot speak for Outdoorsmen generally, but my group is made up of the most fanatic of competitors, all seeking to win points by other means than merely hitting the ball back one more time than the opponent. It is curious to see how certain psychological tactics are translated from summer to winter tennis. There is, for example, the perspiration gambit: in summer, wiping one's hands with a towel after every game, then the racket handle, then the glasses, carefully folding and hanging up the towel, scattering resin on the hands, wiping it off, rubbing the handle with it, blowing it off, etc., etc.; in winter this maneuver consists of removing one's gloves, blowing on the hands, picking up snow and massaging the wrists, spraying some kind of defoggant on the glasses, wiping it off, and then going through the resin bit.

Another one is the inner-temperature–outer-humidity routine: As play progresses, the player removes his heavy outer sweater, then removes the light inner one and replaces the outer one, and, after the next game (or point), puts the inner one over the outer one and shortly afterward, cursing the erratic dew point, removes the outer one *and* inner one and replaces everything with an old army field jacket.

There is an annoying ploy used by Grundy that is good both winter and summer. You serve an ace to him and he continues to stare at you, twirling his racket, crouching in readiness, and shuffling his feet. He does not admit that the ball was in, out, or even that it crossed the net. Finally you ask him if the ball was good. "I don't know," he will say. "I didn't see it." You ask your partner if it was good and he thinks it was. But Grundy's partner thinks it barely missed. There is nothing to do but take the serve over, and by this time your rhythm is broken, to say nothing of your equanimity, and it is inevitable that you double-fault.

A stratagem often employed in summer by Lafferty, but which he cannot make use of in winter, has to do with the court surface. On clay, the ball makes a mark when it lands and if it hits a line some lime gets on it. In summer, if Lafferty thinks a shot of his or his partner's that was called out was good, he will storm over to your side of the court looking for a telltale mark and scrutinizing the ball for specks of white. The purpose of this is to cow you into awarding his team close ones in the future, arouse guilt feelings in you, and shatter your concentration.

Asphalt and cement courts do not record marks made by the ball, however. So in winter, when we play on those surfaces, his tactic is to actually disappear in the middle of a point. During a spirited rally you will suddenly notice that Lafferty's partner is alone on the court. As the action continues, you will catch sight of Lafferty placidly sitting on a bench at the sideline, his racket on his lap. Under these circumstances, if the ball is hit to you, you cannot help but flub the shot. Occasionally, as a variation of the tactic, Lafferty will bound back onto the court like a reserve platoon during a rally, and, due to complete bewilderment, you will probably lose this point, too.

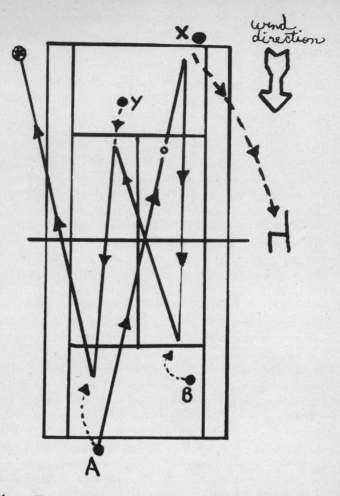

wind direction

Outdoor Tactics II: "The Lafferty Coup"—Server A hits to Lafferty (X), who, after making the return, strolls over to a chair by the netpost and calmly sits down. B returns ball to Lafferty's partner (Y), and Player A notes with consternation that Y is completely alone on the court. What has happened to Lafferty? The shock causes A to drive the ball outside the court and the point goes to Lafferty's team. Nor is Player A much good for the rest of the set.

Two final ploys were recently developed by a psychiatrist in our group who happens to have his own tennis vocabulary. Some times, after you have hit a deep shot, he will call "Back!", probably meaning that the ball struck in back of the baseline. He also hollers "Not!" when a serve is out, presumably meaning "not in" or "not good." In any event, when he makes these sounds it is not your point.

But his main wiles are, as you might expect, psychological. He is an erratic player and when he misses a shot he tumbles into the depths of despair. After missing a series of shots he will wail to you, "I can't hit anything! I'm terrible!" He continues in this vein for a while and then, after repeated misses, suddenly becomes triumphant. "There!" he will announce after putting an easy smash into the net. "I told you I couldn't play this game! I'm rotten!" He shouts other self-damaging phrases as play goes on, becoming happier as the errors pile up. In order to call a halt to this rising euphoria and reduce him to his usual state of gloom and pessimism, you actually have to start missing yourself. Then you can shout back to him, "I'm just as terrible as you are!"

His second stratagem is, I believe, unconscious but nonetheless effective. In a doubles game a short while back, I hit a beautiful forehand drive that soared down the middle and could have landed either in or out. The psychiatrist, after noting where the shot hit, dropped his racket and softly applauded. A little bit later, when I asked him the score it didn't come out right, so we discussed previous shots while my partner and his stood around with their mouths open. The psychiatrist said my forehand down the middle had been out. "But you applauded," I reminded him. "What was that for?"

"It meant the shot was out, and I was happy over winning the point," he said. "The Russians and Hungarians applaud when they're happy."

"And the Eskimos rub noses," I replied, and the next time he ventured up to net I tried to take his head off.

Although outdoor tennis is an immensely complex game, it can be practiced like any other. Here are a few drill exercises for the purpose.

Drills for Outdoor Winter Tennis

1. Serving. Player A takes his stand at the baseline of a swept-off, dried court and keeps tossing up the ball and serving until he gets one in. When this happens, Player B, the receiver, tries to hit it back or watches it go past. Players C and D stand near the net post and share drinks out of a thermos and tin cup.

2. Net Drill. Players A and B get the net from C's car and, against a stopwatch held by D's wife, string it up on two netposts. C and D get the net from A's car and string it up to another net post, timed by a stopwatch held by B's wife. The winner is the team's wife who remembers to push down the little button that starts it.

3. Individual Stroke Practice. If the weather is truly foul and no one else will venture out for tennis, it is a good idea to obtain practice by hitting against a backboard. Equipment needed is a racket, three tennis balls, a snow shovel, and a broom. Telling your wife and whatever company you have you are going to a bar for a few belts, you dress warmly and travel to the backboard. After cleaning away the snow, start stroking forehands and backhands. Try to keep the ball going for at least three consecutive strokes. After ten minutes of this, move in and practice volleys. A good number to shoot for is one, gradually increasing the amount. When you return home, remember to act slightly tipsy.

3

The Great Tennis Specialists

As a long-time player and observer of tennis, I am often asked who among all tennists had, or has, the best forehand, the best drop shot, the most effective second serve, the best developed sense of tactics, and so on. Also, which player would win in a hypothetical match between, say, Billy Johnston and Herb Flam, or Henry Cochet and Pancho Segura; or, in doubles, between Dennis Ralston and Bill Tilden on one side and Clark Graebner and Felicissimo Ampon on the other; or, in mixed, between Jiro Sato and Rosie Casals on one side and Suzanne Lenglen and Charlton Heston on the other.

It has struck me, after many hours of pondering and diagramming dream matches like these and comparing Rosewall's sliced backhand with Budge's topspin backhand (both very neat, by the way), that there is a good deal more to tennis than returning shots, or playing the percentages, or outvolleying one's opponent. Topflight tennis is made up of many elements, a lot of them psychological—concentration, the ability to bluff one's opponent, the ability to make one's opponent nervous or outraged, to name a few. So, instead of comparing classic strokes or matching up Bunny Austin on a damp grass

.court against Wilmer Allison playing on clay, I am going to list the skills and specialties of a few lesser-known but extremely active tennis enthusiasts I am familiar with.

The players mentioned do not have Perry's running forehand or Kramer's mastery of the Big Game, but they are nonetheless very effective, possibly dangerous, competitors because each has developed a unique specialty— a tricky stroke or move or method of attack that compensates for whatever weakness they might have, or, in doubles, that their partner might have. Over the course of the year, indoors and out, this specialty wins them many games and even matches against players who, on paper, might appear superior.

Here are the eight most impressive nonclassic, or neo-classic strokes, moves, and techniques I have seen in the past ten years and the players who dreamed them up. All, I suggest, are eminently worthy of study.

Best Return of Service When the Serve Lands Out

Among the very top players this is not a frequently seen shot; at least it is not considered an essential weapon in their arsenals. Yet Howard Gilchrist of the Van Damm Tennis and Racquet Club in Wampanog, New York, has developed it into an extremely useful stroke.

Gilchrist is normally an erratic player on returns of service when the ball lands *in*. It can fly sideways or straight up in the air or off the throat of his racket. But when the serve hits some little distance beyond the lines, he steps forward and gives the ball a flat, assured crack that sends it whistling back over the net. It is a shot that usually gives the server fits, since, no call having been made by the receiver, he is startled into chasing after the ball.

Gilchrist's return generally goes crosscourt, requiring the server to dash to one side or the other. Then, as the server gets ready to hit the ball, Gilchrist cries, "No!

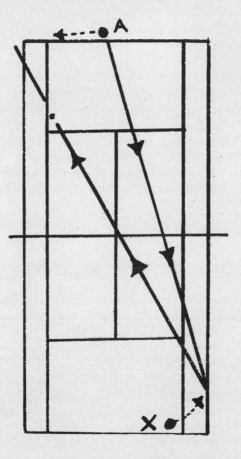

Gilchrist's great return of an out service: Server A hits ball slightly wide of line. Gilchrist (X) slams back a hard crosscourt, galvanizing A into action, then hollers "Out!" after bewildered server has started to swing at ball. Server A will probably double-fault.

That was *out!*"—saving the server from starting his forward swing, or, if he has already slashed at the ball, at least from following through. Then, filled with mixed emotions, the server slowly and sheepishly returns to his position and offers up the second ball, which, you may be sure, has very little bite to it.

Some players, having had unpleasant experiences with Gilchrist's tactic, refuse to chase the ball after he has returned what they presume will be called an out serve even though it appeared to land well in. Gilchrist has an answer for this. He will look surprised and say, "Oh? Did you think that was out? Serve the second ball then." As he twirls his racket awaiting the next serve, I have a feeling that eldritch laughter wells up inside him.

Most Skillful at Upsetting the Rhythm of the Receiver

This is quite different from Gilchrist's great shot, but almost equally effective as practiced by Arnold Justin of the Plainview Country Club in Little Neck, New York. His purpose, when serving, is to throw off the receiver by upsetting his natural rhythm.

When the rhythm of the *server* is broken—as by some interruption immediately after he has served the first ball (like a loose ball from an enemy court bounding across his line of vision)—his opponent, out of courtesy, often awards him two serves. In matches governed by an umpire, the granting of an extra serve in these cases is automatic. But when the rhythm of the *receiver* is upset, no rule is invoked to give him comfort and no courteous gesture is possible. (A server who solicitously inquires, after the first serve has been called a fault, "Were you bothered, old man? I'll take the first serve over," is not helping the receiver at *all*.)

Using his own variation of the Eastern forehand grip,

Justin hits a first serve that seldom goes in if it clears the net but very often hits the tape at the top of the net. There is a sharp, resounding crack in these instances, and because of Newton's Law the ball bounds part of the way back toward him. Justin assumes a distraught look, ponders a moment, then strolls forward to pick up the ball and pocket it. No broken ankles for Justin! This consumes about seventy seconds and is usually sufficient to throw the receiver off whatever is left of his timing. He has to wait, unfocusing his eyes and balancing back and forth on his toes until Justin assembles himself on the baseline and tosses the ball up for his second service, which is a severe slice.

When playing a new opponent, Justin, after hitting the tape with his first serve and watching it bounce back to the middle of the court, will take a halfhearted underhand swipe at the second service ball and send it bouncing along the ground until it hits the bottom of the net. Many players, not knowing Justin, are under the misapprehension that this is a double fault. It is not. It is Justin's way of expressing his dissatisfaction over the bad luck he had with his first serve. Looking shocked at his opponent's double-fault charge, he then retrieves both balls, pockets one, braces himself, and serves his slice. Just as Gilchrist seldom loses games he receives, Justin seldom loses his serve.

The Most Dangerous Service

Everyone knows about the strong serves of Vines, Sangster, Ashe, and Kramer; how Falkenburg won the Wimbledon tournament almost entirely with his serve, and how the left-handed Fraser took the United States title with a similar weapon. I have found, however, that the most dangerous serve—in the game of doubles, anyway—belongs to George Gustafson of the Bay Hills Tennis and Badminton Club in Douglaston, New York.

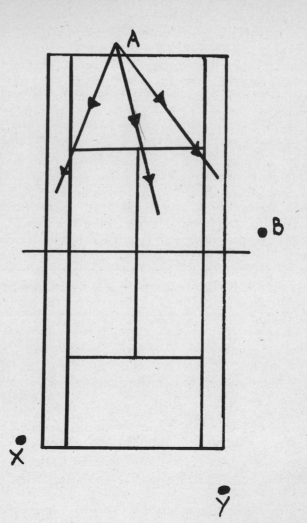

Diagram showing various directions Gustafson's dangerous serve may take when he aims for deuce court, and positions assumed by opponents X and Y and Gustafson's partner B to avoid getting killed.

Gustafson, who hits his first serve flatter and harder than Gonzalez and uses twice as much wrist snap as Laver, is the terror of his doubles opponents when he serves. He scares even his partner.

While the speed of this shot is fantastic, Gustafson is not especially accurate, and if the receiver and his partner are not alert and do not watch the toss, the backswing, the position of Gustafson's shoulders, wrist, hips, knees, and feet as he leaps high in the air to serve and do not duck as the racket is propelled forward, one of them may be in for an unpleasant surprise. Suddenly the ball is a grayish blur that hits the receiver in the foot or knee before bouncing or, more frequently, hits the receiver's partner in the throat or chest before he can dart out of the way. In either case, according to the rules, it is a point for Gustafson's side because the ball hit an opponent before landing in the proper service court. As a consequence, the receiver's partner plays farther back than he would against the average server, while the receiver poises himself several feet behind the baseline—trying to get something between his body and Gustafson, if possible. (Sometimes the netpost and sometimes the umpire's chair act as obstacles.) This naturally opens up many areas of the court for Gustafson's partner at net to attack if the service should happen to land in the proper service box and should by some chance be returned. However, Gustafson's partners are just as terrified as the receivers and generally station themselves somewhat outside the doubles line as a precautionary measure and are seldom in position to handle the service return.

To his credit, Gustafson does not let up on his second serve, should the first not hit anybody or be a fault. It is even flatter, harder, and wilder than the first.

The Most Effective Courtesy Shot

The somewhat quaint name of this stroke—which is used only in warm-up rallies—stems from the fact that it is supposed to be hit so that one's opponent has an easy chance to return it. Ideally, it travels over the net reasonably slowly, bounces gently in the middle of the opponent's court, and presents a likely target for him to swing at.

There is no official rule that says the shot must be a complete setup, however, and there are times in warm-ups when it may be advantageous to prevent your opponent from getting a good crack at the ball—to keep him from finding out what your normal stroke looks like or perhaps to confuse him or make him nervous.

That, at least, is the theory of Ralph Prager, who has developed a very disconcerting courtesy shot indeed. Prager, who is a member of the East Norwich Country Club in New Jersey, drops the ball in front of his right foot, waits for it to come close to the ground after bouncing, and then, with a quick, slashing sideward sweep of his racket—the strings nearly horizontal—puts terrific slice on the ball, sending it skimming over the net and curving it deep to his opponent's backhand corner. On landing, the ball skitters erratically to the right, making it most difficult to return.

Prager can hit the shot with a violent backhand slice, too, dropping the ball in front of his left foot, drawing the racket back behind his right ankle, and sending it skimming off toward his opponent's forehand corner. Sometimes his opponents find themselves racing over to adjoining courts to try to return shots *during the warm-up rally*, which is very difficult to explain besides being exhausting.

When Prager's bewildered opponent retrieves the ball and hits his own courtesy shot, Prager catches the ball, examines it for compression, shakes it for loose things

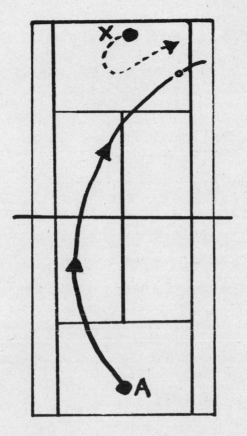

Prager's unreturnable "courtesy shot": To start rally during warmup, Prager (A) drops ball and hits it with fantastic slice, sending it far out of reach of opponent (X), effectively keeping opponent from getting any practice before match.

inside it, and then slices it back with his specialty.

Thanks to a great deal of practice, most often by himself, Prager has developed one of the most unreturnable courtesy shots in the game.

Cleverest at Tempting His Opponent into Error

Everyone has heard of this technique of acquiring points against players of less-than-top rank. When your opponent is in the vicinity of the net, you hit a ball about two feet higher than the tape, slightly out of reach, and with considerable spin. In his anxiety to put away what looks like a sitter (especially if you groan loudly as the ball is about to be hit), he hurries his shot or fails to judge the spin correctly and slams the ball into the net or out of court. Some players rely more on groaning than on spin, and in doubles a good, agonized groan is worth at least one point a game.

Harold Tibby's technique, however, is somewhat different. Tibby, an angular man who plays out of the Memorial Field public courts in Great Neck, New York, tempts his opponent into erring on his *calls*. When he makes a shot that will land very close to one of the lines, Tibby moans loudly (different from a groan), deluding his opponent into assuming that the ball will go out. Hearing these sounds of resignation and despair, his opponent lets the ball go without trying for it. It lands and before he makes the call he glances at Tibby, who, shoulders slumped and racket lowered, seems to have virtually conceded the point. "Out!" the opponent calls, as anyone would.

"What?" demands Tibby, running forward, suddenly full of energy and zeal. "That was *out?* You mean to say you called that shot of mine *out?*"

His opponent, naturally, has to stick to his guns, although on reflection he recalls vaguely that the ball might have landed on the near side of the line rather than the far side—purely a metaphysical distinction but one that disturbs Tibby. Now the opponent is filled with guilt, having been duped into making a questionable call that has been patently challenged. For Tibby has thrown his racket on the court, is standing and staring with his hands on his hips, a look of utter incredulity on his face. His opponent wonders if he will race over to examine some of the marks near the line and claim one of those inside it as his own, or make an appeal to passersby or players on nearby courts to rule on this particular shot. Finally Tibby makes a sound of loud lament to end the dramatic scene and consents to resume play. For the rest of the match his shaken opponent cannot concentrate and loses games he should win. And if Tibby, for his part, calls a few close ones against him, the opponent must keep his protests to himself, apart from casting his eyes skyward and tossing his racket in the air and catching it. The next time Tibby moans as one of his shots soars near a line, his opponent tries to decapitate him with the return, caring little whether Tibby's ball lands in or out. This, too, alas, is Tibby's point.

Doubles Player Best at Protecting His Partner

A rare talent that George M. Lott had to a considerable degree, as did Frank Parker, Bobby Riggs, and Jack Bromwich. If their partners were forced into making a weak return or were pulled far out of position, these players often made spectacular recoveries of their opponent's next attacking shot. The recoveries, frequently hit from off-balance positions, would at least keep the ball in play and on some occasions won the points outright.

Bob Noonan, who drifts from club to club but mainly plays at the Berkshire Hunt and Tennis Club in Flushing, New York, which has two indoor courts, protects his doubles partners in a somewhat different way. When his partner receives service, Noonan, a left-court specialist,

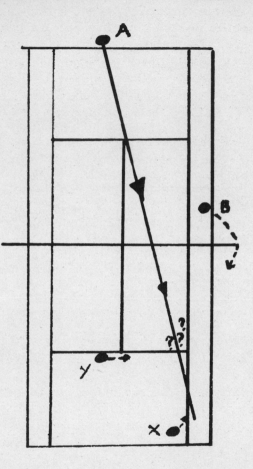

How Noonan protects his partner: Server A hits a hard serve, which Noonan's partner (X) misses. Noonan (Y), moving quickly to right, then declares serve was out. Argument with net man (B) follows, which Noonan wins. The entire procedure adds little to the server's equanimity.

stations himself close to the right rear service line. As the serve is hit, Noonan follows the ball closely to determine precisely where it lands. If it is good and his partner hits it back, Noonan says nothing. If it is out and his partner hits it back, he says nothing. But if his partner misses and there is some question as to whether the ball landed in the proper service box, Noonan announces that the serve was out. The following discussion, or one reasonably close to it, usually takes place:

SERVER: Did you call that out?

NOONAN'S PARTNER: I didn't see it. It could have been out.

NET MAN: It was four inches inside the line. I'll show you the mark.

NOONAN: I'll show *you* the mark. It was out. I had a good look at it.

SERVER: Well, how do you want to call it?

NOONAN'S PARTNER: My partner says it was out.

NOONAN: Oh, it was out.

SERVER: Well, how do you want to call it?

NOONAN'S PARTNER: I guess it must have been out. Just missed.

NOONAN: Hit your second serve.

NET MAN: And for God's sake, don't come near a line.

Noonan also helps his partner when a shot lands near the baseline or a sideline that his partner misses. He has an authoritative, reassuring voice that brooks very little argument, particularly during late-at-night indoor matches when everyone's resistance is low and the opponents do not want to waste their money arguing.

To his credit, when Noonan himself misses a shot near the line he never makes a bad call, although he may turn to his partner with a look of great sincerity and ask if the ball was barely in or slightly out. His partners, sadly, do not give him anywhere near the support they should.

Best Player at Making His Opponent Take the Far Side of the Court

Strictly speaking, this is not a tennis stroke, any more than Noonan's method of protecting his doubles partner is a tennis stroke. But it is a useful tactic in obtaining a psychological advantage over one's opponent at the outset of play, provided he happens to be aware of the significance of the move.

In most cases, it is traditional for the inferior of two players to take the far side, though there are some exceptions: A youngster playing an elderly gentleman would take the far side; a male player hitting with a female other than his wife would take the far side; a guest playing on a private court at a rich man's estate would automatically, and cheerily, bound over to the far side. These are conventional courtesies. But when players are roughly equal in age, use club or public courts, are of about equal ability, and neither owes money to the other, both engage in a variety of subtle maneuvers to seize the near side.

Since it is accepted that the less skillful of the two players is going to make the long trip around the netpost and to the distant court, it follows that the player who sets out on the trip—or is duped into making it—is admitting that he is the inferior player. This cannot help but affect the way he plays the match—and, indeed, all future matches with this same opponent. For if you once accept the ignominious role of trudging to the far court while your opponent preens himself and relaxes on the near side, you are likely to make the trip more passively each successive time.

The player who I think is the world's best at this meneuver (I have never seen anyone take the near court away from him) is Charley Sykes. Sykes, a stocky man with a red face, is not a very good player, but he takes games and even sets from better players (such as Arnold

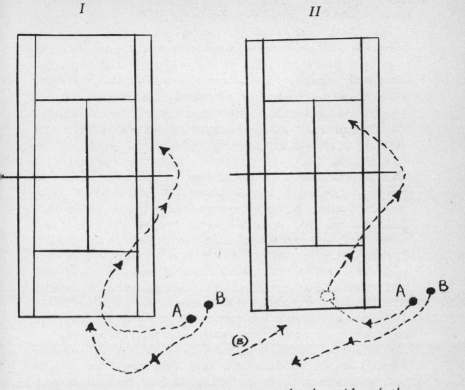

Getting opponent to march over to the far side of the court before play I: As opponent (A) starts for near side, Sykes (B) manages to stay behind him and to the outside. Before opponent knows it, Sykes is so far back that opponent must take the far court, a psychologically upsetting experience.

Getting opponent to march over to the far side of the court before play II: Against an opponent who defiantly positions himself on the near side, Sykes (B) uses a different tactic. He disappears until opponent takes the far side, then suddenly reappears and triumphantly takes the near-side position as opponent steams.

Justin, who belongs to the same club) merely because of his extraordinary mastery of this tactic.

Sykes knows many tricks. The basic one is to plant himself on the outside of an opponent and keep about three respectful paces behind him. To save time, the opponent reasons, he should take the far side because he is several yards closer and, no matter how slowly he walks, Sykes keeps losing ground. Some opponents (especially those who have beaten Sykes in tennis the week before) feel that Sykes should acknowledge their superiority by taking the far court. They walk extremely carefully, as though on hot coals, trying to edge between the fence and Sykes. But Sykes counters this by hugging the fence and even pretending to peer through it, as though tennis was the last thing on his mind. He even manages to take a few steps backward while appearing to walk forward, like a man learning the rumba.

If an opponent grimly takes the bit in his teeth, marches forward, and firmly stations himself in the middle of the baseline of the near court, defying Skyes to dislodge him, the champion relies on one of two basic maneuvers. The first is casually strolling to a point between his opponent and the fence and calmly waiting while bouncing a tennis ball. Since it is clear that the opponent is nearer the far court than Sykes, he must eventually lose patience and storm over there. Or Sykes will say to the implanted opponent, "Oh, excuse me! I have to see the pro about my strings." And he will vanish into the clubhouse, remaining there until his opponent, having nothing to do, starts practicing serves. When the opponent walks over to the other side to hit serves from there, Sykes appears, all smiles and waving his racket as he takes the near court, apparently delighted with the stringing job. As well he might be.

The Most Brilliant Strategist

You can talk all you want about the tactical virtuosity and courtcraft of such as Whitney Reed, Manuel Santana, Pancho Gonzalez, Art Larsen, and Bill Tilden—players who could wrong-foot and confuse their opponents, keep them off-balance mentally, disguise shots, do the unexpected, outmaneuver and outguess their opponents, and sooner or later break up their games. But give me Clarence Olsen every time. He is not a truly great player, or even a good one, but he is a deep thinker with great powers of concentration. What is more important, he is a busy strategist off the court as well as on and he utilizes his acumen in a very special way.

Clarence's main trouble is that his wife will not let him drink. This is partly because of a few unfortunate things that have happened to him at social gatherings, in the bar car of the commuter train, in cocktail lounges, at weddings, office parties, class reunions, and so on. His superego takes over after several nips and he makes a lot of noise and breaks things, tears clothing, spills drinks, challenges friends and strangers (of both sexes) to fight, drives like a maniac, and so on. Like many athletes, he relishes a little libation after strenuous exercise, feeling he deserves it, but his wife hides the liquor in his home, even the vanilla. And since she handles the money he does not carry any cash with him when he goes out to play tennis—except for a dime for a phone call, maybe—because she does not give him any. Nor does he dare cash a small check somewhere that would at some future date cause a disturbing interrogation because he has a low threshold of decibel tolerance and his wife conducts her queries in a screech without pause for any answers.

However, a great thirst inspires ingenuity, and a couple of years ago Clarence came up with a splendid idea that keeps him comfortably drunk over part of the weekend during the tennis season—which, indoors and out, lasts about eleven and a half months.

What Clarence does is use his immense brainpower in this way: He enters dozens of tournaments—indoor, outdoor, guest–member, local, special, over–thirty-five, over–forty-five, singles, doubles, mixed doubles, handicap. It is all a big mystery to his wife, who does not understand why Clarence, who has not a single trophy, is so bugged on playing in tournaments. What she does not know is that in tournaments of these types the rule says that it is up to the loser of a match to furnish the balls. That is, after the match, the player who has furnished the balls keeps them if he loses; if he wins, he gives the loser the balls and accepts the loser's can of new balls. In most cases, the inferior or more pessimistic player furnishes the balls to save a lot of trouble; often, in the early rounds of a tournament, the "superior" players will not bring cans of balls at all. These are meat for Clarence.

A few days before his match he calls his opponent and, after setting the time and date, assures him that he, Clarence, will be happy to furnish the tennis balls. He indicates by his tone and a few apologetic phrases that he does not expect to win—lack of practice, arthritic twinges in his back, shoulder, and elbow, unfamiliarity with the court surface, a two-year layoff, and so on. After a phone call like this, some opponents line up a tough practice match to follow Clarence immediately because they feel he will throw them off their game for weeks.

Clarence's appearance as he steps on the court supports this. He wears shorts too large, a red-and-blue-striped T-shirt, basketball highs, and black silk business socks. His racket has a busted string. Both knees are encased in surgical bandages; he once played a match with a soft cast on his elbow. When he rallies he can hardly reach the ball, much less return it accurately, and during the match he smokes part of a cigarette while changing courts.

As the set progresses, however, his opponent becomes

aware that Clarence never double-faults, never misses a shot in the vicinity of the backcourt, hits sky-high lobs that bounce over the fence when he is in trouble, and puts tricky left-handed spin on his slices.

When the match is over, with Clarence winning about 6–3, 6–2, the business of the loser furnishing the balls comes up. Since his opponent did not bring any, it is only courtesy that he should pay Clarence in specie. This is pure cash profit for Clarence because he obtained his can of tennis balls by charging them at the local drugstore. (The drugstore does not sell liquor or his wife would not let him have a charge account there.) So Clarence, apologizing for the upset, pockets the $2.30, congratulates his opponent on some of his great shots, and makes off for the nearest pub. There he can get three whiskies and four beers and have a nickel left over. Most bartenders will fill your beer glass if they see you are serious about hoisting a succession of boilermakers, and there is also the tradition of a free whiskey after three have been purchased. So Clarence gets comfortably loaded—though not enough to hit a cop—and returns to the courts to hazily watch a few matches to get a line on future opponents and then saunters home.

He manages to put together about two or three binges during the course of an average tournament; then he meets a top-ranking player like Gilchrist or Justin, who makes use of his own psychology, and takes his shellacking, winding up with nothing but three old, abused tennis balls.

But as long as overconfident opponents last, Clarence, head abuzz, happily saunters home, where the business of opening the front door tends to sober him up somewhat. If you do not stare at his reddened eyes, listen too closely to him, or get too near him, you will never believe he has had a drink. Coaches know what they are talking about when they tell you if you do a particular thing often enough you get to be an expert at it.

49 · *The Great Tennis Specialists*

There you have them. Put these eight players together, with all their special skills, and you create the "dream player" who will never lose a match—if he can find some-one willing to step on the court with him.

4

Some Queries Answered

As you might expect, it is not unusual for me to be the recipient of letters asking questions having to do with tennis—rules, knotty problems, stroking, equipment, history, and so on. With the hope that some of these questions and their answers will be of interest and help to the avid player and spectator, I am setting them down below.

Q.: When do you shout the term "not up" to your opponent?

R. B. J., Chicago, Ill.

A.: After he has moved forward on a low ball and hit a shot that gets by you but is so far in that you do not dare call it out.

Q.: What is the advantage of running forward to take a high lob before it bounces instead of after?

O. H. W., Fort Worth, Tex.

A.: You get two swings at it.

Q.: Where should I play if I have a bad backhand?

W. B., Cheshire, Conn.

A.: At the Wampahonsset Country Club in Wampahonsset, New York.

Q.: What happens when a shot hits the umpire?

G. M. H., New York, N.Y.

A.: He starts to pay attention to the match.

Q.: How do you keep score when your opponent is slightly deaf?

R. W. T., Niles, Mich.

A.: Loudly.

Q.: My smash, which I hit with a Continental grip, usually goes to the forehand of my opponent. What should I do to make sure it goes to his backhand?

A. S., Great Neck, N.Y.

A.: Play left-handers.

Q.: This question about rules concerns a doubles match between A and B on one side and C and D on the other. During an extended rally, A hits the ball to C, but before C can get to it, Player E, from an adjoining court, sidles onto C–D's court after a stray ball and, in a fit of whimsy, makes the return. Unfortunately, it is a weak lob that B smashes out of reach. C and D scream that this is interference, but A–B claim the point, saying they had momentum. No umpire was present to make the decision, so what is the proper ruling?

R. K. A., San Diego, Calif.

A.: The accepted ruling, in the absence of an umpire, is that the player who struck the ball during the period of alleged interference can argue that the point should be played over. Since E hit the ball, it is up to him to conduct the argument, although he may have long since lost interest.

Q.: What is the best way to disguise my backhand?

O. J. S., Berkeley, Calif.

A.: Hit it off the forehand side.

Q.: Is there any difference between red and white tennis balls?

P. G. D., Seattle, Wash.

A.: I presume you are kidding.

Q.: Is it considered courtesy if I ask a player worse than I am to play with me?

H. K., Philadelphia, Pa.

A.: Yes, if you can find one.

Q.: What would happen if Whitney Reed met Frank X. Shields?

U. W. H., Newark, N.J.

A.: They would probably go somewhere and have a drink together.

Q.: What happens in a tournament match if the vertical belt holding the net breaks?

H. W. S., Butte, Mont.

A.: The net blows all over the place.

Q.: When should I go in after my serve?

R. G., Massapequa, N.Y.

A.: *Never!*

Q.: Is a "net ball" the same as a "let ball"?

M. C. R., Baton Rouge, La.

A.: To a lot of people, apparently.

Q.: What is meant by a "good loss"?

H. D., Kansas City, Mo.

A.: When you lose but your opponent is so sore, beat up, exhausted, and nervous from winning that he has to go to bed for a week.

Q.: How can I keep my feet from "burning" when playing on a hard surface, such as cement?

W. D. I., Newton, Mass.

A.: By wearing some sort of foot covering, such as sneakers.

Q.: What is the record for consecutive double-faults in a single game?

F. McV., Bangor, Me.

A.: Five—held by many players, including several of my doubles partners.

Q.: How high would a regulation pressurized tennis ball bounce if dropped from the top of the Empire State Building?

O. A. F., Erie, Pa.

A.: Depends on who you hit.

Q.: Where should I serve if the sun gets in my eyes?

G. D. V., Tallahassee, Fla.

A.: Northern Sweden.

Q.: Could you please tell me the names of the famous "Four Musketeers" of France?

L. D., New Orleans, La.

A.: Certainly. Athos, Porthos, Aramis, and later d'Artagnan.

Q.: In doubles, what is a good percent of getting your first serve in?

R. B. D., Ames, Ia.

A.: 100.

Q.: Would it help your game if you chinned yourself six times a day?

L. W. H., South Bend, Ind.

A.: I am not even going to try.

Q.: Is it permissible for the receiver, after his opponent has served one fault, to carefully remove and hang up his sweater?

J. H., Merion, Pa.

A.: Can you think of a better time?

Q.: In serving in doubles, what happens if my racket flies out of my hand?

P. W. D., San Francisco, Calif.

A.: You scare the bejeezus out of your partner at net.

Q.: How can I keep my opponent from lobbing over my head?

M. C. S., Cicero, Ill.

A.: Stand two feet behind the baseline.

Upsetting the Server

Q.: What is the best reply, in singles, to a hard, high-bouncing American Twist serve hit to the backhand with terrific spin? In doubles?

W. S., Manchester, Conn.

A.: (1) "Close!" (2) "Let my partner call it."

Q.: Is it possible to put downward slice on a backhand return when using a Western Grip?

W. G. C., Sussex, England

A.: Yes, but you will break your wrist.

Q.: What should I do if my forehand sails?

W. B., Port Washington, N.Y.

A.: How about investing in some new tennis balls?

Q.: Since you are a tennis expert, I have a few questions for you that came up in our annual club tournament recently. (1) After A has served one fault at 15–40, can B ostentatiously move forward to the edge of the rear service line to intimidate him? (2)If a ball is terrifically undercut and bounces first on the opponent's side of the net and then on your side and then back again, who is supposed to hit it, or who is entitled to hit it? (3) If both players hit the net simultaneously in going after a lob, who is awarded the point? (4) If two linesmen disagree on a particular shot—whether it hit the edge of the line or not—can one of the players make the call? If so, which player? (5) If the players forget to change courts at the end of an odd-numbered game and the umpire overlooks it, can Player A demand that the set be started over again? (6) How many tosses is the server allowed to make before he must swing at the ball?

W. M., Douglaston, N.Y.

A.: Go to hell.

Q.: If my backhand is very bad and my overhead is almost useless, on which side of the court would my partner prefer that I play?

J. K. F., Hightstown, N.J.

A.: The other side.

Q.: Does the winner or loser buy the drinks after the match?

K. M. M., Hollywood, Calif.

A.: Your opponent does—whether he wins or loses—or there are no drinks.

5

Sounds and Countersounds

The game of tennis is filled with sounds, many of them joyous: the fffFFFFFSSSsss of somebody else opening up the can of balls he is supplying that you are about to play with; the glorious exploding reverberating *pop!* of a flat-hit forehand when you are playing inside an inflated balloon while the fierce myrmidons of winter are clashing outside; the delicious brief but unmistakable *klk* of one of your shots hitting the line tape in your opponent's court—which means you have aural as well as visual evidence that the shot was good; the pervasive tearing, crunching, echoing clang when a lob sent up by one of your opponents strikes the joists, purlins, beams, and light fixtures overhead, saving your partner the trouble of having to smash the ball into the net.

Even silence can be joyous, as when one of your opponents serves the first ball into the net tape, watches the ball roll back toward him, and evinces growing anxiety as he realizes that neither you nor your partner, conspiring beautifully, are going to give him the serve over just because his rhythm, if it can be called that, has been broken.

However, there are other sounds that can be distinctly disturbing, as most of us are well aware, and the majority

58

of these, if not all, emanate from the human larynx and thorax. Some of them are involuntary, caused by the pressures of competition, and some are not.

But just as the deep topspin drive can be countered by a chopped lob, the spin of an American Twist removed by hitting flat through the ball—on paper, anyway—and a clever drop shot defused by an even cleverer one, so the sounds made by your opponents—as likely to break up your game as any stroking tactics—can be rendered less effective by what might be called Countersounds. Here they are.

Opponent's Sound	Countersound
When you hit your first serve and it either whistles past your opponent before landing out or hits the net tape with a deafening crack, he goes "Whew!" somewhere up in the treble register in an awed way. This means he is terrified of your serve, so, after brief reflection, you hit the second one even harder. I defy anyone under these circumstances to do anything but double-fault.	You drop your racket, pause, and repeat "Whoooo-ooo? What does that mean? Are you giving me the serve over? What's the score anyway? (*to net man*) Should I be serving, George? (*after net man gives you perplexed look*) These balls seem dead to me. Do we have another can?" (Even if your opponent does not give you the serve over, you will at least have recovered enough poise to carefully guide the second serve into the service box.)
"*Oh, Willie!*" This could be any name, but it erupts from the striker who suddenly berates himself for having	On hearing the cry you return your opponent's weak lob with an even weaker one, and, just before he hits it, holler out

Opponent's Sound

hit a shallow lob that
invites an unreturnable
smash. The anguish of his
tone fills you with guilt
for taking unfair advantage
of a despairing opponent,
so you hesitate for a split
second before regathering
your resources, then hit
the ball with the edge of
the throat of your racket,
sending it 50 yards
sideways.

When a high-bouncing
short ball looms up for you
to clobber, one of your
opponents cries to his
partner, "Cover the alley!"
You, the striker, become
confused by this because
you don't know if an
opening exists, or did exist,
or will exist,
or which alley will be
covered if you should go
for the opening—assuming
that the ball goes
approximately where you
intend to direct it. Or if
it is all some kind of sly
trap. So you hit a tentative
shot while glancing at the
moving figures across the
net, and, if your shot
happens to go over, it is

Countersound

your own name in a
reprimanding voice filled
with the agonies of hell. If
your opponent has any
compassion whatsoever,
his eyes will bug out and
he will hit the ball over
the rear fence.

As the sound is made you
step in and, forgetting the
alley, slam the ball hard
at whatever opponent is
close to the net and, if the
shot is successful, make
the sounds of apology to
the victim clutching
himself. "I thought you
were covering the other
alley," is the best
explanation to offer as he
staggers away, rolling his
eyes and getting ready to
play the next point.

Quieting a Noisy Player

an easy putaway for
the other side.

After missing a shot—
hard, easy, or medium—
some players feel impelled
to put on a dramatic
performance of
self-castigation and
remonstrance that would
outshine John Barrymore
as Mercutio in *Romeo
and Juliet*. Viz.:

Oh, you idiot! Missing
that easy shot. You didn't
bring the racket back. You
were off-balance. You
failed to look at the ball.
You didn't follow through.
(*Raps racket hard on
court.*)
You're not playing your
usual game.
Take your time and crack
the ball. An-ticipate.
You've got to get ready
sooner, hit through the
ball—ah, ah, ah (*practicing
forehand swings*).
Concentrate! Relax!
Firm grip!

The cry wells up after
every shot the player
misses—that is, three or

Before serving to this
gentleman following one of
his outbursts, you stand
behind the baseline, then
move the front foot
backward and begin to
declaim in a loud voice:
"Oh, you miserable lout,
why are you standing
there when you know you
should be two feet to the
right and facing the
sideline instead of the
net?" After walking around
in a small circle, you move
to the proper site, then
toss the ball up as though
to serve and let it bounce.
"Oh, you stupe," you
berate yourself, "why do
you toss the ball up like
that when you know it
should be tossed higher
and more forward so you
can put more wrist into the
shot? You didn't brace
your feet, you held the ball
too tight, you didn't release
it soon enough, your
fingers weren't relaxed
enough, you didn't bring
the racket back far enough
or out enough or up enough

Opponent's Sound	*Countersound*
four a game, more in deuce games. Eventually becoming sympathetic toward or alarmed over this visible disintegration of a human personality, his opponents find themselves giving him shots they hope will provide some measure of therapy and wind up losing the set.	or time the swing right." Three aborted serves accompanied by critiques of varying degrees of severity should be good enough.

These countersounds should be practiced at least twice a week, in a vacant lot and in bad weather, if possible. Sincerity is important.

6

Doubles Troubles

Doubles is a game fast growing in popularity—especially with the boom in tennis played on indoor courts, where only a millionaire or the owner's in-laws can afford to play singles. I have played a good deal of doubles myself, indoors and out, and like, I imagine, the majority of doubles players I have mixed feelings about the game.

It is true you don't have to run as much as in singles, the strategy is more profound, and there are longer rest periods between points while players are trying to figure out who is serving, who is receiving, where the balls are, and so on, but the big trouble in doubles is that you are playing with a *partner*. And this makes it something of an ordeal. You have little or no control over this man—his mental outlook, quirks in his personality, his tendency to collapse under pressure, or his concept of tennis tactics (unless he is amenable to advice) and other things.

A good partner is the sine qua non of playing competent doubles because it is essentially a game of position, concentration, and keeping the ball in play. Flashy strokes, useful in singles, are best kept at a minimum, since, if they do not come off, they lead to long dissertations interesting only to the player whose brilliance has resulted in a lost point. Personally, I am a very patient tennis player, except when somebody does not know what the score is (or gets it wrong!), but in my doubles career I have had some lulus as partners—players whose on-court conduct would make a Billy Budd blow up and lose concentration. Here are some of them.

First there is the partner who keeps tossing asides at you about how well one of your opponents is playing. "He's really hitting them today, isn't he?" he will say after the opponent has made a routine smash of a low lob your partner has sent up. Then, "You know why he enjoyed making you miss that shot so much? Because he hit the kind of soft 'nothing' shot you usually hit and you couldn't handle it." Inspiring.

But even worse than this type of partner is the one who compliments an opponent *during a rally*. Not long ago I played a match on a badly lit indoor court with a stage producer for a partner who apparently needed a lot of legal advice. Our opponents were a judge about seventy years old and a trial lawyer about fifty. In one game I hit a beautiful short shot with lots of sideward spin that the judge lunged for and managed to scoop up and plunk back. "Beautiful shot, Alec," my partner enthused, moving up to a tactically disastrous position between the baseline and rear service line as I knifed the ball with backspin directly at the judge's feet. Somehow he got his racket on the twisting shot and half-volleyed it back. While I was slicing the return with a kind of half-overhead to the lawyer, my partner called, "What a terrific shot, Alec!" The lawyer thereupon stuck his racket in front of the ball and hit a setup to my partner—always dangerous for my side—and he promptly knocked it far out of court. Feeling exactly like Spartacus at Cannae (or wherever it was he discovered he had an extra enemy), I completely lost my concentration, and there went the game, the set, the match, and any chance of meeting Anne Bancroft.

Then there is the partner who gives the opponent who is serving an extra serve. Sometimes it is inevitable that a serve comes so close to the line that you automatically return it and, after the server or net man makes his volley, quietly inform him that the serve was out. This should not disturb him unduly if he has any kind of tennis sense; he should go back and promptly serve the second ball. But sometimes your partner, in a spirit of magnanimity or for some other inscrutable reason, will call to the server, "Take two, please."

Now what the devil right does he have to allow the server to take an extra serve *in your court*? Let him have the server take two, or even three, serves in his own court if he wants, but the service box for which you are responsible should be inviolate. What happens is that you are forced to overrule him. "Take one, please," you call in a tone that indicates he is lucky to get even *that*.

While I am on the subject of magnanimity, I have had partners who would literally say, after dumping the return of service into the net, "My fault." Or flubbing the simplest of smashes: "My fault." Who else's fault would it be? Charles de Gaulle's? I am waiting for some partner to hit two serves into the back wall and acknowledge, "My fault." It is the recurring memory of fatuous statements like this from your partner that causes you to blow an easy setup at the net *four games later*.

This is not an act that sends me into convulsions, but it is nonetheless very annoying: the business of your partner costing you an extra serve. After the receiver has hit your serve back, calling it out, he catches the ball with great agility and stashes it in his pocket, then resumes his crouch at the net. Whereas if he had any brains he would let the ball go by, allowing you to make a great show of running to it and hitting it back (no matter how much screaming your opponents were doing that the serve was out), and then look so confused that your opponents would have to give you the first serve over. But it is hard to register confusion when your partner has simply pocketed the ball and is calmly waiting for you to deliver the second serve. Fortunately, the receiver will probably tear his head off with the return, which may teach him a lesson.

Add to these the partner who makes witty comments about your coordination and strokes. After some error of yours he will call jovially to your opponents, "Roger reminds me of that graceful bird, the elephant." Or, "He reminds me of somebody I saw at Forest Hills—the guy that runs the tobacco store." Or, to you after a shot of yours has sailed far out of court, "Nice hit . . . But the wrong game." Or, after a ball has skittered off the throat of your racket, "You paid for the racket, you might as well use all of it." Or, after you have unintentionally hit a shot with the frame that has won the point. "Good miss!" Or, after you have hit the first serve out, from his position at net, "One fault coming." Or, if you serve without the style of a Sangster or Trabert, "Roger is the only player I ever saw who ran around his *service*."

Then there is the partner who plays close to the net on your first serve but timidly retreats to the baseline just before you toss the ball up for your second. Even worse is the partner who stands just behind the baseline no matter which serve you are hitting.

Sometimes an opponent will hit a shot so high and hard that it looks as though it will sail out. If my partner looks as though he is going to hit it, I quite properly holler "No!" in a tone so loud that he is immediately frozen into inaction and the ball goes on its merry way. But I have had partners who called, "It's going to go out. Let it go!" By the time they get to the meat of their oration you are making your follow-through, somewhat shakily, and the ball has long since landed in the middle of the net.

I had one partner, a player named Walter, who destroyed me with a single word. A short lob was coming down, and just as I was about to put it away, Walter, who was standing somewhere behind me, hollered "Shift!" in my ear. Not only was I terrified by the noise, but I suddenly wondered what he meant by it—this while I was swinging at the ball. The instruction could have been in-

terpreted several ways, all of which were academic, because no player in the world could have hit a successful smash with Walter shouting "Shift!" in his ear. After the ball was relayed back—it had sailed on a line parallel to the net, hitting a player five courts away—I asked Walter what he meant. (It might have taken me longer to say it than that.) He said he meant that after I hit the smash I should have shifted to a particular side of the court because he had planned to shift to the *other* side of the court. Whether he meant right or left I do not know, because I broke my racket on the netpost in frustration.

I have had some extremely casual partners, too—players who don't mind missing easy shots and gradually working your side to that terrible situation when one more point will give your opponents the match. Presumably they are not trying to make you explode with their nonchalance, but that is the effect they have. There was one partner who, nearly every time he missed a shot, would remark, "Good idea—poor execution." Another partner had a habit of hitting balls that would have gone out, whether I yelled at him or not. His comment was, after losing the point, "I came to play." Another partner I was blessed with played abominably for the first five games of the set despite all the instructional help I could give him. At that point he said, "I think we throw each other off." I went into a state of shock at the comment and was not much good for the remainder of the match.

Some partners disrupt your concentration by their odd habits. I played with a man from the Southwest who wore a Stetson hat and, when he was about to receive, called out "Deal!" to the server to indicate he was ready. I suppose if he was playing stud poker he would say "Go ahead and serve" to the dealer. Another partner I briefly had never used to tell the server whether his first serve was in or out. Instead, he would raise his left hand, palm up, and signal with his fingers in a kind of impatient "come forward" gesture—the way you would indicate to a truck driver he could come ahead several more feet before going into a ditch. After a while you learned he meant the first serve was out and that the server should deliver the second ball. He was a member of that small group of players who fortunately are as upsetting to their opponents as to their partner. I had a psychiatrist as partner once who played very well for three games and then completely went to pieces. After the set, which we lost, he apologized for the way he had played. "I couldn't hit a thing," he said. "One of my patients was watching."

There is one player I have been assiduously avoiding as a partner because, although I am reasonably well-controlled on the court, I think after the first two points I would kill him. This is a player about my age whom I refer to as the General because he believes he knows so much about tactics and, no matter how experienced his partner is, continually gives advice and barks orders during the play of a point.

"What did you do that for?" he will demand after his partner has hit a lob down the middle. Then, after he makes a return himself, he calls, "Get up to net! They've got to hit a defensive shot!" Holding himself in reserve about a yard in front of the baseline, he masterminds the attack. "Firm wrist! . . . Don't hit to Fred! . . . Back up, back up! . . . Now, *that* was a silly shot . . . If it comes back, cover the middle . . . Move up—too far! . . . Backhand! . . . It's going to be good. Play it! . . . Don't hit it there! . . . Watch out—*backspin!* . . . Do you see it?" (This refers to a lob the General himself has hit and which has presumably soared so high it baffles human vision.)

If the General loses the point, it is because his partner did not follow tactical instructions; if his partner loses the point, the General analyzes at length what he did wrong. And God help you if the General makes a placement. It is Tannenberg all over again. Naturally, the General plays a lot of singles.

I do not expect a partner to hold the net down for me when I serve or anything like that, but here are the things

I believe the Perfect Partner (as near as it is possible to get, anyway) should do:

If he makes a mistake about the score, it is always in your side's favor.

He gets as enraged about shots of yours that your opponents call out as about shots of *his* they call out.

If you call a ball hit by your opponents out, he supports you enthusiastically or, to avoid a whole lot of confusion, keeps his big mouth shut.

He does not hide a ball in his pocket.

He gets his first serve in 15 percent of the time; does not double-fault on match point.

He does not object to a touch of color in his partner's apparel.

He supplies the balls at least 20 percent of the time.

He knows who is receiving and who is serving at least 60 percent of the time.

When you miss a shot, he listens intently to explanations about the lighting, the bounce, airplanes.

Limits his own explanations of missed shots to 30 seconds.

Tells the ladies on the next court to shut up—saving you the trouble.

Wants to celebrate victories in a festive way after the match is over.

Unfortunately, I have never met anybody like that and I don't expect I ever will.

Let me conclude this on a light note. I once had a partner on a hot day who, during the change of courts, asked me if he could use my towel. "Sure," I said. "Go ahead." So he blew his nose in it.

7

Quiz for Tennis Experts

(Note: By "expert" is meant a thinking player who relies on stratagems and guile as much as on powerful strokes and sharp volleys to confound his opponent and in some cases the umpire.)

1. After a long rally, your opponent finally hits a desperate shot that lands in the vicinity of the baseline, causing little cumulus clouds of lime to rise and hang suspended in the air—this despite the fact that you know in your heart that the ball was out. In view of the circumstantial evidence that the ball was good, how do you inform your opponent that his shot was out?

a. "The wind took it out. Look how it's blowing the chalk up!"

b. "Boy, are you having rotten luck with the lines today!"

c. "Tough."

d. "A half-inch closer and you'd have made it."

2. The main object of tennis is not necessarily to win but to impress the audience that you are much better than you appear or the score indicates. While losing badly to a player you consider inferior, you miss an easy shot. How

do you indicate to interested observers that you are playing a great deal below form?

a. Throw your racket down, fling your arms in the air, and cry out, "Would you *believe!*"

b. Turn to the audience and calmly confide, "It's difficult getting used to clay after the grass at East Orange."

c. Pick up one of the balls and with your best shot hit it far over the fence.

d. March to the sidelines and ostentatiously break your racket.

3. When you are serving in doubles, what is the best way to keep your partner from overambitious poaching at the net—that is, hogging every ball that comes near him and piling up errors for your side?

a. Request that he stick to his own side of the court.

b. When he serves, go for every ball that comes back over the net.

c. Suggest to the opponents an immediate change of partners.

d. Hit him in the back of the head with your serve.

4. In indoor doubles, one of your opponents hits a high, deep lob that you thought would go out but which, in fact, appears to have landed six inches inside the baseline. What is the call you make?

a. (*To the striker*) "Would you mind calling that? I was watching the ball, not the line."

b. (*To both opponents*) "Believe it or not, that was close enough to be called in."

c. (*To your partner*) "I'll let *you* call that one."

d. (*To the pro, if nearby*) "The lighting is terrible in here."

5. A basic stratagem in tennis is to upset your opponent when the opportunity arises. What is the best way to do this if, after he serves a fault, his second serve lands too deep and is also a fault?

a. Catch the ball and announce: "Double-fault."

b. Hit a beautiful forehand back, then announce: "Double-fault."

c. Wind up, take a terrific swing at the ball, deliberately miss, and announce: "Double-fault."

6. You happen to be umpiring a match between the monarch of a European kingdom and an archduke on one side and two ranking American amateurs on the other. At the end of a brief rally, the archduke questions you about a shot hit by the king. Give the proper reply.

a. "That shot was out, Your Grace."

b. "That stroke missed the line, Your Excellency."

c. "Unfortunately, Your Imperial Dukedom, the shot was hit too deeply."

d. "His Majesty's shot overextended itself."

e. "Out."

7. In a match your opponent blatantly foot-faults—that is, places one foot or both feet on or inside the baseline before striking the ball—every time he serves. In the absence of an umpire and linesmen, how do you call this unfair practice to his attention?

a. Holler "Foot-fault!" every time he tosses the ball up.

8. Before an early-round tournament match, played without an umpire or linesmen, your opponent comes up to you in a chummy way and says, "We'll call our own double-hits—okay?" This means:

a. That he is scrupulously honest and expects you to be the same.

b. That he does not know what a double-hit is.

c. That he constantly double-hits (and does not wish this to be called to his attention).

d. That he is trying to upset your concentration.

9. While trying to pass your opponent at net, you hit a

hard, deep shot. Judging from his cry of "Just out!", approximately where did your ball land?

    a. Three inches beyond the baseline.
    b. One inch out.
    c. Two inches in.

10. In a tournament match supervised by an umpire, your opponent hits a ball that strikes the top of the net and bounces in your court, but the umpire calls the shot out, giving you the point. What should you do?

    a. Insist that the point be played over.
    b. Quietly throw the next point.
    c. As a humorous gesture, remove your glasses and offer them to the umpire. (If you do not wear glasses, forget it.)
    d. Rest easy in the knowledge that the umpire is there to call the shots impartially and it is about time he called one your way, meanwhile suppressing all temptation to spot the expression on your opponent's face and giggle.

Answers to Tennis Quiz

1. c. Anything else will make your opponent think you have a guilty conscience, and he will begin to mistrust your judgment on *all* shots that cause the chalk to rise.

2. d. Especially if you happen to have an extra racket.

3. d. The first serve, as that is probably not going to go in anyway. If you hit him with your second, he may not even be aware of it.

4. None of these. e. (*To partner*) "I thought the damn thing hit one of those girders up there on the way down. How did it look to you, Harry?"

5. None of these. d. You calmly watch the ball sail back to the fence and, after retrieving it, announce the score incorrectly (40–30 for 30–40, say). Your opponent will glow, thinking he has served an ace. Just before he serves again you announce the correct score and tell him about

the bad news on the previous point: "Oh, that was way out." After a meaningful pause, you should be rewarded with another double-fault.

6. None of these. f. "Both your opponents called the royal shot good, Your Grace, and so did I. It is a placement for His Majesty, and I am so marking it in the royal archives."

7. a. The only conceivable remedy.

8. b, c, d. If your answer was "a," you have no business on the tennis court.

9. None of these. d. Ten feet out. He was being sarcastic.

10. Are you kidding?

Scoring: If you got 1–6 right—beginner; 7–8 right—O.K. player; 9 right—true competitor; 10 right—can play in my group.

8

The Seven Toughest Tennis Courts

If you know anything about sports, you know that because of varying topography and climate all over the world, plus the ingenuity of links architects, all golf courses are supposed to be different. There are sandy courses, concrete courses, grass courses, courses with lots of trees, courses specializing in water holes, courses where the player who hooks has an advantage over the player who sclaffs and vice versa.

About twice a year it is the habit of golf experts to list and describe the five or ten or fifteen toughest golf courses they have played on. Or they back into the subject by recalling and comparing the holes they consider the most difficult—the sixth at Pine Valley, the eighteenth at Pebble Beach, the eleventh at Soundview, and so on—no two on the same course, naturally.

If golfers can write about unusual golf courses, it would seem to follow that a tennis player, such as myself, can write about unusual tennis courts, and I have compiled a list of the seven most unique, picturesque, and devilishly difficult courts I have played on.

To the casual observer it might seem that all tennis courts are identical—they measure roughly the same, the

77

surface is reasonably flat and level, and the only hazard is the net. Nothing could be further from the truth.

I can tell you, as varied and eccentric as some golf courses may be, they are not a patch on the immense variety of tennis courts currently in use. These include private, club-owned, public, indoor, outdoor, inside inflated balloons, hollowed out of warehouses, converted from printing plants, on rooftops, on cliffs, on marshes, all-weather, and bad-weather. Then there are the numberless types of surfaces: composition, concrete, weeds, cork, linoleum, carpeting, plastic, wood, and others. Not only does a ball bounce differently on these different surfaces but on some surfaces it never bounces the same way twice. Plus there are differences in color; the effect on the court of weather; the clarity of the lines; the *shape* of the court, by God; the height of the ceiling overhead, if indoors; proximity to an aerodrome and popularity with lady doubles players, if outdoors. Wind affects a tennis ball more than it does a golf ball. Some courts give the advantage to a left-hander, some to the hyperkinetic player who hits the ball with all his might and dashes up to net. How close a surrounding fence hugs the court vastly affects play (as we shall see). Some courts lie so close to each other that, in trying to retrieve a wide-angled shot, a player can risk injury from another player *two courts away*. Tennis courts change from season to season—soggy, cracked, scarred with heelmarks, smooth, rough, slippery, sandy in some places, rocklike in others. Light and shadow, such as caused by moving leaves, clouds jumping in front of the sun, the state of the equinox—all these affect the play of each point. A tennis player has got to be constantly improvising.

When you think about it, all a golfer has to worry about, from the standpoint of losing concentration, is crowd noises, somebody's shadow crossing the line of his putt, or whether he is using the right club. But the tennis player, hitting a moving ball while he himself is in motion and in a position of great mental strain, has a much more difficult task.

I do not mean to put down golf as a sport, but any damn fool can hit a stationary ball while he himself is standing still; but the tennis player, scampering around the court, has to judge the flight of the ball, remember how old the balls are (age affecting the bounce), if all the balls used are uniform, how his own spin is going to counteract the spin on the ball, what the score is (determining whether he is going to hit a textbook shot or merely try to get the ball back), and what his partner is doing, plus putting together about twenty different elements involved in making even the simplest stroke. In addition to all that, he has to worry about whether his opponents are likely to call the shot out or not. It is clear the pressures are tremendous.

Here, then, are my choices for the seven toughest tennis courts in the world:

The first is a private court, used only for singles, owned by Al Bailey of Teaneck, New Jersey. Bailey is left-handed and, like all left-handers, reaps all the benefits he can from this unnatural condition. His court, designed by himself and a monstrosity of engineering, gives him an immense advantage. Bailey's serve happens to have considerable slice, the ball skidding far to the left after it bounces, looking like nothing so much as a small, rapidly accelerating hen's egg. But it is not so much the spin that is troublesome, nor the surface of the court (it is glassy smooth), but the arrangement of the fence. This is how the court is set up:

The diagram makes it clear that Bailey, when he serves to the ad (or left-hand) court, is able to curve the ball into the fence after it bounces and before the receiver can get to it. Even if the receiver could squeeze himself between the ball and the fence, he has no room to swing the racket. From a statistical standpoint, therefore, Bailey can do no worse than tie, even if his opponent was Bobby Riggs. He

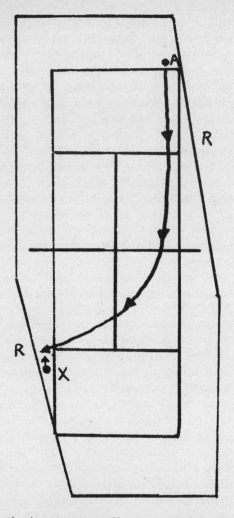

Bailey's Strategically Designed Court
A—Left-hander Bailey Serving
X—Unfortunate Receiver
R—Wire Fence

wins every point in the ad court and eventually he is going to win a point in the deuce court. Since he wins all his service games, he is sure to win every set, even if it goes to 34–all. Sooner or later the grimmest adversary is going to crack. Right-handers strive mightily to serve the ball into the fence, too, but the court was not built to their specifications. You can double-fault an entire set away before you give him trouble. The best I have been able to do is carry him to 16–14, and I had a raw shoulder afterward.

Thanks to the special nature of this court—the only place where he will play—Bailey has not been defeated in the past eighteen years except by his twelve-year-old daughter, who also happens to be left-handed.

As practically everyone knows, the major world championships—Wimbledon, the National Doubles at Longwood or Chestnut Hill, the National Singles at Chestnut Hill, the Australian championships, and a few others—are played on grass. I have never played in any of these tournaments, but I have played a good deal on grass and I know how treacherous it can be. The ball bounces so low you have to hit a lot of scoop shots, and if you are headed in one direction you have to keep going that way or you will fall down or twist something. Naturally, you get tangled up in the net a lot.

But the worst grass court I ever played on is owned by Albert Souzery de la Foulet, a marquis, or so he claims, who lives just outside of Westbury, New York. Since it is a private court, it seldom gets the attention of, say, the center court at Wimbledon. The surface, consequently, is composed of swatches of bent, clover, crabgrass, bluegrass, fescue, dandelions, and many other unclassified types of lawn phenomena, all differently affecting the bounce. The marquis has a cousin—an earl, probably—who mows the court every Sunday in the summer, so if you play on Monday you are all right. But if you play after

Tuesday you are in trouble, because the grass, weeds, and fungus all grow at different rates.

I seldom do well on this court, because I do not care much for going to net, but that is where points are won. They are lost by letting the ball bounce. After it hits it can rebound any one of six ways, the favorite one being a little bit backward and off to the right. But the most interesting feature of the marquis' court is that one part of it was built over a cesspool that was filled in about sixty years ago, and it is slowly sinking. After a heavy rainfall the filled-in part retains all the moisture, and it is a desperate player indeed who will venture after a lob or groundstroke into "the marsh," as this section has come to be called. A ball on landing there usually burrows itself into the ooze and has to be lofted out, like a golfer extricating a ball wedged in a bunker—except that your golfer has all the time in the world, whereas the tennis player while pursuing the shot is always waiting for his opponent to scream "Not up!" if he does not get there quick enough. Once during a doubles tournament—the championship of North Teaneck, held on the marquis' court—a player lumbering after a lob sank to his knees in the quagmire. He miraculously made the return, but when he was plucked out by his partner and a linesman after the point his shoes had disappeared and they have never been seen to this day. Given new shoes, he finished the match, but his concentration was broken and the marquis and his partner retained their title, which they will probably continue to do every year the tournament is played in April.

Number three is one of the five courts at a ritzy Long Island private club I used to belong to—the most northern, Number 5. The courts were clay and kept reasonably smooth, being ready only three days after a rainfall, but the caretaker who lined them was sometimes affected by the summer heat. His name was Augustus and when he returned a ball to you if he was lining one court while you were playing on another, he would kick it over or, in the manner of a soccer player, toss it up and hit it over with his head. I don't believe he ever had any profound knowledge of tennis.

Augustus would start out early in the morning, all efficiency, but when noontime came round the heat made him feel quite jolly. Since it was his summer habit to nap from two to six on the days he lined the courts, he had a tendency to hurry when it came to lining Numbers 4 and 5. Between his difficulties with getting the strings and stakes aligned and following the sometimes erratic paths of previous lines, the last two courts took on a kind of irregular, jagged appearance. Psychedelic, people would call them nowadays.

Naturally, the club's best players always commandeered the first three courts, but often—as for tournaments— Numbers 4 and 5 had to be used by both the great and small. The smart player assigned to one of these would study the vagaries of the lines before getting into action, pointing out to his male or female partner that there was a bulge on the right side of the doubles sideline opposite the service line on the side of the court facing east; that when serving from the east into the ad court you had an extra two feet of space to put the ball in if you served to the backhand; when playing on the western side you should expect arguments from the opponents when one of their shots landed near the baseline on the forehand side because, out of whimsy or because he had lost the remains of his coordination, Augustus had serrated this part of the baseline like the blade of a saw; that when playing the western side a lob to the opponents' forehand side was a dangerous shot because Augustus (in a hurry to get to the clubhouse for refreshment, probably) had so severely angled the baseline that a huge area of the opponents' court had simply vanished. These represented the major variations on Courts 4 and 5—especially 5 (see diagram). Meanwhile, the server on the eastern side, when he served to the forehand court, could make excellent use of the proximity of the baseline to the net. Aces were relatively routine.

I won several trophies on court Number 5 and not a one on the others, showing that there is more to tennis than just slamming the ball hard and racing like Lochinvar to the net. Unfortunately, Augustus got a job with the state road commission laying down the lines dividing lanes in highways, a complete teetotaler replaced him, and I have not won a trophy since.

In the course of playing tennis in many climes and latitudes, a player encounters many diverse and challenging personalities—some of them quite famous. In the Los Angeles area I have played against several actors and in Beverly Hills I played doubles against two Australian players fresh from triumphs at Forest Hills and Longwood..The match took place at the posh George Klabish Tennis Club, in many ways the most ideal place to play tennis in North America.

The eight courts are immaculately kept, the surface an easy-on-the-eyes grayish-blue composition—part cork, part carpet—reverently rolled twice a day, the lines freshly covered with lime every morning and swept every time an important match is to be played. The fences are well back, allowing one room to cover lobs without fear of injury. Behind each court is a comforting natural green background of trees, hedges, and grass. For singles matches, so conscientious is Mr. Klabish's pro, Arnold Farr, that net sticks hold up the net on each side, creating the proper slope and height. The clubhouse itself is luxurious, even by Hollywood standards, and a good many golfers are being wooed away from that game to take up, or at least watch, tennis. The way it is played at the George Klabish T.C. it is far more exciting than golf and lends itself even more enthusiastically to that sine qua non of Hollywood athletic diversions, betting. An interesting sidelight is that no members of the club are allowed to buy life insurance.

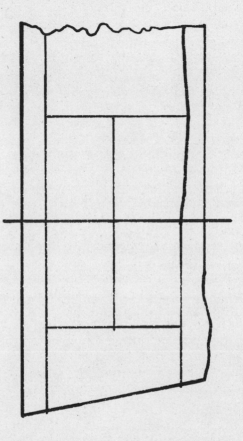

No. 5 Court at ritzy Long Island tennis club as lined by
Augustus on a thirsty day.

Most of the betting is done on matches played on the so-called Handicap Court—Number 3. This court, directly in front of the wide clubhouse patio, differs from the others only in that there is a thick post about four feet high midway between the T formed by the service lines and the baseline on the patio side. It is called a tethering post, goes underground a solid fifty feet, and is used in some matches to keep large animals, like elephants, from wandering over onto nearby courts and, in some cases, to limit the range of contact, so to speak, of a carnivore on one side of the court.

The post was erected in 1955 after a near accident frightened many spectators out of their wits. A famous movie star, since divorced, had challenged Klabish—then the Minnesota Fats of tennis pros—to a one-set match for a five-thousand-dollar side bet. Klabish was, of course, much the better player, so the actor was accorded a handicap. The stipulation, thought up by the actor, was for Klabish to be fastened by the left wrist to the right front leg of an elephant. Klabish readily accepted, the bets were recorded, and the menagerie under contract to the actor's studio furnished the elephant, a female named Betsy.

The match started out as might have been expected, with the actor hitting shots to Klabish's backhand, where he had to duck under Betsy's front legs to return the ball, or wide to Klabish's forehand, where he had to coax and tug the 4,200 pounds of pachyderm toward the sideline by his wrist. But with the score 4–2 in Klabish's favor— mainly by virtue of unreturnable services and topped drives to the actor's backhand—Betsy got sick of being hauled around so capriciously by this nervous biped and trotted off the court despite George's wheedling and the shouts in Urdu of her mahout. Unfortunately, she chose to run onto the court where the finals of the mixed doubles were being played. The ladies ran screaming off the court, along with the linesmen, while the male players, having reputations to uphold, hid under the grandstand. Betsy trumpeted, fluffed out her ears, tried to shake

Klabish off her leg, and made a mess of courts 5, 6, and 7. Meanwhile, Klabish's opponent, the famous actor, was trotting after Betsy, trying to get Klabish's attention and demanding to know if Klabish was going to forfeit. Upset, his wrist sore, Klabish hit him with his racket.

Eventually Betsy got tired of all the brouhaha and lay down on court Number 8, where the nearby trees are thickest, and fell into a doze. Klabish shouted for the mahout, who had been under the grandstand, and he finally appeared with a kris and cut Klabish loose. About an hour later a menagerie van appeared, and, lured by eucalyptus leaves, Betsy was coaxed into it and sped away to her Burbank home. Two days later the tethering post was set up.

On another occasion Klabish was challenged to a different kind of contest. This actor said that Klabish did not have to wear a suit of medieval armor (as he has done) or play lefty (you never know with Klabish) or carry a starlet on his back for a set (as he has offered to do) or tie himself to an animal.

Klabish wondered what the gimmick was. It turned out the actor wanted to tie a wolverine to the post, giving Klabish a certain amount of room to operate in, but Klabish would have to take his chances when he went after shots near the center of the court. A four-foot tether was agreed on, a seven-thousand-dollar even-money bet was registered, and the match was on.

The wolverine happened to be in bad spirits that day, and Klabish lost four straight points as the actor kept drilling shots to the center of the court. After a few brushes with the wolverine, Klabish decided to concede all points involving a death risk. When the game was over, the actor began to chortle confidently in front of his lady friend, the wife of an aging child star, and then looked surprised as Klabish walked toward the netpost. "Where are you going?" demanded the actor.

Klabish, the veteran hustler, smiled. It seemed that the rules called for the players to switch on odd-numbered

Playing with a Handicap

games (something the actor had not given thought to), and now suddenly the actor would have custody of the wolverine. He argued passionately for fifteen minutes but finally had to accede. Needless to say, as games were played, as strategy was employed and courts were exchanged, the score rose to 13–all before it was apparent that neither player could win a game in the wolverine's court. Neither was going to risk being clawed or bitten (or sued, if the wolverine should bust a tooth) for a mere seven thousand dollars. So the match ended in a tie, with the honor of both parties satisfied.

This brings us to my own match on the Handicap Court at the club—one of the most unusual in Southern California history. Klabish (playing left court) and I (right court) were paired against two top-ranked Australian Davis Cup players. The atmosphere, as you can imagine, was electric. The only stipulation made by my side was that the Australians were to play wearing slalom skis— easily obtained at a downtown Los Angeles department store. The tethering post was an additional handicap for whoever court it was on, something like one of those squatty little posts in skittles.

Having to serve from four feet behind the baseline on account of the tips of their skis and falling down a lot in their efforts to retrieve Klabish's topspin lobs as well as my own carefully blocked returns of service, the Australians found themselves in terrible difficulty and finally lost 9–7. I understand quite a bit of money changed hands after the set. I wish to hell I had bet.

Court number five on my list is also in California. It is owned by an actor so famous he must be referred to only as Mr. T. To keep from being mobbed by fans, hangers-on, and agents, he lives in a palatial aerie overlooking the Pacific just south of Big Sur and he chose to have his tennis court constructed on the steep cliff close by his residence. Wealthy actors, like generals, want to cut off as many approaches to their fortresses as possible, which is why you find their homes surrounded by impenetrable forests on two sides and things like an insurmountable cliff on the other. Anyway, you can hear seagulls screaking and the ominous thunder of waves crashing on the rocks a quarter of a mile below—something like the opening shots of a Hitchcock movie. It is all very scenic and profound if you do not have to play tennis there.

I have never seen a profile of the declivity making up the actor's backyard, but I imagine that the wave action, the force of gravity, corrosion, and other natural forces have pretty will hollowed out the precipice so that it must be shaped like a U lying on its side. One-half of his tennis court projects out over the hollow part while the other half rests on relatively firm ground.

As a result of this whimsical layout, the player on the far side constantly worries about landslides, washouts, subsurface faults, and the like, taking care not to slam down his feet too hard on that part of the court nearest the baseline. In chasing down a lob, there is a wire fence to keep you from plummeting down onto the rocks below if you should be too zealous in your attempt to retrieve it, but most players on the cliff side of the court readily concede anything that sails over their heads and is apt to land in as the opponent's point. Actor T., who has long arms and spidery legs, is well aware of his opponent's trepidation, of course. His favorite tactic is to hit the ball deep to his guest's backhand and storm the net. All that is missing are the bugle notes for the cavalry charge. As you pound after the ball and assemble yourself to hit it, you cannot help but wonder if the ground is going to crumble away from under your feet, leaving you awash on the rocks at the mercy of the squawling gulls. If anyone can hit a shot past T. under these circumstances, my hat is off to him. When T. takes the precipice side of the court (you change after each set), he spends all his time up at net, where he is on relatively solid ground. All his opponent has to worry about is attacks by hovering seagulls. The only possible way to beat him, I have figured, is to get

Playing on an Actor's Court

so completely sozzled at his playroom bar before stepping onto the court that you forget all about the cliff, the rocks, the crashing surf, the looming presence at the net, and natural erosion. But then your accuracy would probably suffer.

By far the ghastliest tennis court I ever played on (it is indoors, naturally) is located right in the center of one of America's largest and most cosmopolitan cities. It is one of a battery of four courts, all pretty much alike, but differing from the two end ones in that vertical green nets separate it from the others on both sides, as opposed to walls bordering the end ones that keep you from running onto the street. Since the four courts take up space that would normally be just right for two and a half courts (the site is a converted printing plant), the hanging nets come in handy. Despite certain inconveniences, because of the boom in physical fitness and especially indoor tennis, the courts are always crowded with doubles groups. I understand some players actually spend New Year's Eve there, playing tennis while having a snort or two. It is more expensive than going to a nightclub, but you don't have a bad hangover the next day—although you might have a few bruises and perhaps a leg fracture and a mild head injury from the general congestion.

The motif for the courts is different shades of green. I think P. K. Wrigley must have been the designer. Either him or H. P. Lovecraft. The surface is a gravelly green substance, and the lines are light green. The balls start out white, but after a few games they begin to match the surrounding walls, which closely match the court. Your sneakers and socks take on a greenish hue after a while, and if you should fall down you come up like Jonah emerging from the whale and wearing the same kind of expression. The nets separating the courts, obtained from the tuna merchants of Sardinia, are likewise green. They are held up by clotheslines about eight feet off the floor.

Around the court you can hear a mysterious chirping

and twirping which you become used to after a few sets. If you look hard you can make out a pipe affixed high up on the wall where the sounds come from. The pipe has little gas flames inside it—presumably to take the chill off the place in winter; they certainly do not add much to the illumination. The pipe itself is a light chartreuse.

After entering the building, you walk down an absolutely pitch-black alcove to reach the locker room, feeling your way with your racket. The management keeps saying it is going to install a light there, but I am sure something (like a zoning regulation) will come up to prevent it. The locker room is lit by a pair of 15-watt bulbs too large to fit into a pocket flashlight, and sometimes a man with an acetylene torch adds to the illumination while he is attacking a row of lockers.

The purpose of all this attention to off-court lighting, I imagine, is to give you the impression, once you step out onto the court, that the courts themselves are brightly lighted. The management does not fool *me*. The lighting, from overhead, is greenish-blue and very eccentric in that it seems to flicker on and off every millisecond or so—something like a fluorescent kitchen light down to its last 500 lumens. My theory is that two squirrels on a pair of treadmills are the source of the electrical power. One of my witty advertising friends has likened the court we use to Boris Karloff's driveway. Another player—unknown—once wrote on the locker room wall, "Mushrooms, yes; tennis, no"—a bit of graffiti that was soon expunged, you may be sure.

When you start playing you find you can hardly distinguish your opponents across the net in the sepulchral atmosphere, and the ball coming at you looks vaguely like a meteorite until it crosses the net. The worst thing about the court though is that any angled shot—such as a crosscourt drive—has to be returned with a volley, or, in chasing it, you get tangled up in the vertical nets, at the risk of breaking your ankles, knees, or racket. Naturally, everyone tries to hit crosscourt drives. Even if the opponent returns it, his partner has to cover the entire court while he examines himself for broken bones, extricates himself from the net, and hobbles back onto the court to resume play. I have played on this court a few times when one of the regular members of the foursome had the flu or a twisted tibia, and it is quite an experience. Fully half the points have to be replayed because players from courts on each side continually invade your territory, clad in the ghoulish green nets and trying to return the ball and fight their way back to their own court; also because the macabre lighting and matching shades of green everywhere make it difficult to say whether a shot was truly in or out or what. I have seen players bend over a line after a point holding a lighted match, trying to find the mark the ball made. (Needless to say, when they found it the call went against their opponents.) And also because of balls from other courts banging against the low ceiling's even lower girders and rebounding onto your court, interrupting play—often to the relief of the weary competitors. Sometimes if a replayed point ends too rapidly—by the delivery of a service ace, for instance—the winning party feels guilty and the point is played over once again. If a set goes to 4–all within a two-hour period, you consider yourself lucky. I am always grateful if a week passes in the winter and nobody asks me to fill in. It is three days before I can face a piece of chewing gum.

The last court on my list is even more challenging. It is what is called an open-air roof court on top of a 25-story building facing the Loop in Chicago. The surface of the floor was originally pine covered with a thick-napped carpet, and some very successful lawyers had their offices there. Then suddenly the lawyers disappeared, and an enterprising businessman bought the entire floor and, after some litigation, got permission to erect two tennis courts. So he tore down the walls, sold the carpets and what was left of the files, removed the roof, covered the pine with fast-drying cement, strung up two nets, and started a private club for businessmen. They generally play during lunchtime—1:00 to 4:30—or after work—from 3:00 P.M. on. I was invited to play there three months ago.

The bounce of the ball is reasonably consistent, and there is space enough behind the back line to return lobs if you can manage to do it without a backswing, but, because of prevailing winds off Lake Michigan and certain meteorological conditions, plus the effect of surrounding buildings and heat rising from the streets, the flight of the ball is affected by downdrafts, updrafts, heat rising from below, low pressure areas from North Dakota, and combinations of these phenomena that seem to affect the vertical as well as the horizontal flow of the air. It is very hard to follow the ball in flight.

Even in tossing up the ball to serve, the player is likely to find it coming down ten feet in front of him, six feet behind him, or floating a tantalizing ten feet above his head and refusing to come down at all. Smashing is impossible because most of the time the ball does not come down, or comes down sideways, or two balls come down simultaneously (one from the point played previously). Sometimes you feel you are playing inside a Time Tunnel.

An additional mental hazard is the fact that once a ball is hit hard and high over the surrounding walls, it is lost forever, landing on State Street to the surprise of pedestrians or in Lake Michigan or somewhere. The first time I played on these rooftop courts I hit four successive forehand drives over the wall and into the metropolis below before I got the hang of the bounce and the wind currents. Then it was about one per game. (You have a fat chance of getting the balls back from lifeguards or pedestrians, incidentally.) However, I look forward to being invited back.

I don't think you will find any tougher courts than these seven.

9

Preparing for the Tournament Match

Sooner or later the time will come, as it must to every man, when you have to play a match. The tournament you signed up for so blithely in July has finally gotten underway in August. The drawsheet is posted, the tournament committee has extracted your two dollars to help pay for the trophies, the seeded players have been accorded their prestigious positions, and your name has been set down next to that of a stranger. A time has been set, by one device or another, for you to play the match on an upcoming Saturday afternoon.

A tournament match, even for the most experienced player, is not like a "fun game" or "social tennis." It is deadly serious. It is official. The result is stamped on the records. It may be watched by spectators who are awed by the tension. The players' behavior must be circumspect. People will talk about the match (maybe not yours, but *some* match) for weeks, maybe years. The local paper will chronicle it for all to read. Those who did not witness it are at liberty to speculate when they peruse the result posted: "I see Charlie choked." "Bill must have pooped out in the third set." "Andy must have talked him out of it." "Who the hell would have thought Carlos could lick Enright in a tournament?" "Hugh wouldn't have got past the first round if it wasn't for the defaults. He must have made the draw himself." "I see Mort choked." Chuckles, nudges, gasps, smirks among the noncompetitors.

The match—confrontation with a stranger from a strange tribe—*mano a mano* combat at its most primitive, involving guile, speed afoot, stamina, valor, composure in the face of bad calls, large portions of what Hemingway termed grace under pressure—this naturally creates a certain amount of anxiety in the mortal so committed. The greats of tennis—Vines, Budge, Kramer, Stoefen, Savitt—all these players felt nervous, some even ill, before a tournament or Davis Cup match. Also Barrymore on the stage, Alex Karras in football. The club player and weekend player, in similar circumstances, have got to be similarly affected.

Tension mounts as the day and hour approach. Your arm feels heavy, you have no feeling in your fingers. Twinges develop in critical joints. Your breath becomes short and your heart gives a leap when you think of stepping into the arena and playing that first vital point. Your palms are clammy and your insides feel funny.

In the days preceding the match you look for signs of a spell of wet weather or hurricane that might postpone the thing. You await with increased anxiety the phone call that (hopefully) tells you that your opponent wants to put off the encounter or (glory be!) for some reason has to default. You find yourself barking at waiters, the boss, lifeguards, and others. You practice forehands (racketless) while walking down the hallway, leading the secretaries to think you are crazy.

Your daydreams concern disaster: inability to get the serve in the proper box; the haunting specter of a tall, angular man who cannot be dislodged from the net; facing a player of indomitable patience who returns everything like a human backboard. At night in bed you are beset by sudden fears—that a huge crowd, composed in part of your opponent's relatives, will attend the match and make unpleasant noises when you call one of his shots out; that your faceless opponent, having seen you play, has spotted your weaknesses, if any (ha, ha), and has engaged a pro to practice those shots that will take best advantage of them. You sit up sharply, wide-awake. The *fiend.*

Days you find yourself doodling stratagems—bring him up close to net, send him back, then slap a fast crosscourt shot that even Bitsy Grant couldn't reach. Deep to the backhand, short to the forehand, deep to the backhand. Impossible angles that make the spectators goggle. Wrong-foot him, trick him with spin, murder his second serve. His tongue will hang out.

You also become concerned with the state of your physiology—each separate tendon, ligament, and capillary. If somebody shakes your hand too enthusiastically, you withdraw quickly and eye him with dismay. Later you solicitously examine your fingers. You refuse to arm-wrestle at parties. You constantly clench and unclench your fingers and swivel your wrist—partly to condition them for the ordeal ahead and partly to see if they still answer summonses from your brain.

When you take a drink it is with the consciousness that you are helping yourself relax from the terrible burden you are carrying, that you are deriving further tactical insights and are building up a calorie bank for that awful time in the middle of the second set when you will have to call on all your reserves to chase down a lob for a critical point.

Naturally, you play a lot of tennis: well-thought-out practice matches with tough players to improve reflexes and endurance; matches with poor players to build up confidence and experiment with new tricky strokes; mixed doubles so you can bask in the glory of the gladiator about to venture into the arena; men's doubles so that you can hone an edge to your hostility.

However, other preparations are essential if you are to

give the best account of yourself possible. You have got to take care of your general physical condition, your hand-eye coordination, your mental alertness, and, in particular, your equanimity. The sooner you start, the more you will improve, or, looking at it negatively, the less you will deteriorate.

A month before the match is not too early to begin serious training, increasing its vigor as the day of the match approaches. Naturally, all players are not of the same ability or temperament, but here is a recommended program that might be followed to advantage by almost any player entered in a tournament:

One Month Before

No reading
No washing dishes
No lifting heavy objects
Jog 100 yards

Two Weeks Before

No household chores of any type
No discussion of personal finances
Don't do anything foolish
Six kneebends

One Week Before

No driving
Do everything left-handed (if right-handed)
Don't run with a stick in your mouth
Reduce smoking by 35 percent
Check over equipment (rackets, Sweatlets, etc.)
(If in doubles tournament) Call partner once an even-

ing to plot strategy, discuss opponents, encourage each
other
    No TV news shows
    Check drawsheet to see if opponent has defaulted
    Do wind sprints of ten yards (two)

Three Days Before

    Check with phone company to see if phone works (op-
ponent may have been trying to reach you to postpone
match or default)
    Don't pet any strange animals
    Check weather reports
    No fried foods
    No discussion of match with family unless you initiate
it
    Walk away from conversations about politics
    Refrain from calling opponent to ask him if he wishes
to default

One Day Before

    Cut down on drinking
    Check the mail (to see if opponent has gone to Ber-
muda)
    Reduce smoking to 25 percent
    Call meteorologist personally
    Call tournament director and ask him if he has any
news for you
    Go to neighbor's house and phone home to see if incom-
ing calls come through
    Recheck equipment
    Call number-one seeded player to find out if there is
anything you can do about your backhand
    Take two salt tablets

The Tournament Player

The Day

    No drinking
    No arguing (before the match)
    No unnecessary steps or other movement
    Take deep breaths
    Send wife to look at drawsheet (in case opponent has defaulted)
    Let hands dangle loosely
    Lie down with feet in air
    Send wife to look for postman (in case opponent is in Quebec)
    Recheck equipment
    Dress carefully
    Place cocktail glass in refrigerator
    Five minutes of rock 'n' roll show on TV (to get psyched up)
    Go!

I have been talking about equipment. In a tournament match, of course, you will need more equipment than in a friendly one, partly because of the pressures and partly because it would be disastrous to be caught without a vital tool at a critical time. I myself have sorely regretted not having a visored cap during a drizzle and, on a very humid day, not having a fluffy towel to wipe off the racket handle. Not all of the equipment listed below is essential for every player. For instance, in doubles maybe you can borrow a piece of gum from your partner (do not ask him after the match); nor will you need suntan lotion on a cloudy day. On the other hand, I have not listed items like surgical bandages for physical or psychological reasons, feeling that is up to the individual. The items should be carried in a large bag rather than loose and it might be effective if the bag had certain foreign labels on it, as though you had played in these countries, like a skier's patches on his jacket. Do not expect the labels to win the match for you by themselves, however.

Equipment for Tournament Match

Band-Aids
Adhesive tape
Cotton
Half-pint of vodka
Gum
Cough drops
Aspirin
Cap with long visor
Dark glasses
Extra glasses
At least two extra tennis rackets (not in the bag, stupid)
Handkerchief
Orange slices
Salt tablets
Miltowns
Stickum for racket handle
Towel
Extra towel for partner (if doubles)
Sweatlets
Extra T-shirt (change after first set to boost morale)
Extra pants (in case first pair breaks)
Rulebook with certain passages underlined
Wax for glasses (in case they steam up)
Green visor
Cigarettes
Extra shoelaces
Tourniquet
Kleenexes
Dime
Liniment
Small pair of scissors

Suntan lotion
Cold cream
Ascorbic acid tablets

Optional Equipment

Toupee
Empty bottle of white shoe polish (see what follows)
Good-luck charms
Smelling salts (for partner, if doubles)

After arriving, checking the drawsheet, locating your opponent, scrutinizing him for bandages and signs of weakness (and undergoing a scrutiny yourself), you chase some players off a court in a self-righteous way and set down your equipment and rackets. Now begins the warm-up—one of the truly critical elements of tournament-match play. Its objectives are fivefold:

To rid yourself of nerves before actual play begins
To get the feel of the surface and the bounce
To determine what you can about your opponent's game
To keep your opponent, insofar as possible, from getting any practice
To keep your opponent from learning anything about your own strokes

The first three aims need no explanation, but the last two may. Keeping your opponent from getting any practice involves hitting a few balls into the net, a few behind the baseline, and the rest at such sharp angles that if he returns one he is in no position to return the next. Also putting terrific spin on some shots so that they bounce crooked and fly off in all directions after he hits them. And when he is at net, either trying to kill him with flat drives or chasing him back to the baseline with deep lobs, apologizing profusely all the while.

What makes this difficult is that all the time you are doing it you must disguise the way you really play. Because while you are sizing him up, he is sizing *you* up—how you hit forehands and backhands, how you volley, how you move, how deep you hit the ball, what kinds of shots give you trouble. Therefore you should do everything backwards. If you are frightened to death of playing net, trot up there and make some volleys. When you miss the ball he will think you are not warmed up yet. Practice a few serves and follow them to net. (Don't get exhausted, however.) If your best shot is a chop, hit drives flat and deep—to the back fence if you have to. If your game is largely endurance and patience, pretend you are out of condition and recommend a rest after the warm-up. Never hit two balls back in succession. If your best shot is a topped forehand, change your grip and slice everything. If your backhand is strong, lead him to think it simply does not exist by continually running around it in alarm. When you practice serves, hit a reverse twist. If you hit drives off the back foot ordinarily, hit off the front foot.

You can imagine how his stream of consciousness is flowing as he watches you play: "Oh, boy. All I have to do is hit the ball to his backhand and it's a sure point . . . My God, he'll break his wrist if he hits a shot like that . . . What does he do when I hit a ball right at him? . . . Panics . . . This guy is going to be some competition! . . . How does he handle spin? . . . Misses the ball entirely . . . File that fact away. I better remember not to win too big or my next opponent will break his neck practicing . . . My God, what a forehand. He must have been bedridden for the past three months. (*Exchanging looks with spectators and shrugging*) My God, I didn't make up the draw . . . Another ball over the fence. Well, he hit it, let him figure out how to get it back . . . Now for some net . . . Oh, boy, three straight lobs over my head . . . So much for net practice . . . And to think I passed up a big party last night!"

Then, the moment the match gets under way, off comes

the disguise, you quickly shift gears into your usual game, and your opponent, suddenly disillusioned, will play the first set in a state of shock. But after that you are on your own.

There are times, naturally, when you want to intimidate the hell out of your opponent; that is, play the part of the casually optimistic expert, indicating by various subtleties that such matches are a daily occurrence with you. This deception is a useful device when you suspect that your opponent is so good that ordinary machinations will not work, or when your opponent is so cocky that you must jolt him into a semblance of reality; or when you are short on practice and have such a miserable hangover that you cannot hope to control the ball the way you usually do.

If you can frighten your opponent before the match by displaying the symbols and accoutrements of skill and experience, he may choke or become perplexed or lose some of his gall—in which case you will do better on the scoreboard than if you played it straight. Here is the method:

For two weeks prior to the match practice bouncing the ball on the edge of the racket when the frame is extended vertically. When you perform this stunt before a match or while waiting to serve, it shows you have good racket control and an excellent eye; that, through usage, the racket has become an extension of your arm; and that you have spent a lot of time waiting for opponents on the court. If your opponent has ever been to Forest Hills or Wimbledon, he will probably recall players of the caliber of Roy Emerson and Gene Scott doing this and he will probably grow nervous at the memory. At the very worst it will keep you from fainting. You might shop around for a racket with a large flat outside frame for just this purpose.

Next, buy five new racket covers bearing the name of some tennis-equipment manufacturing firm like Dunlop,

Wilson, or Slazenger (all the same, of course). You can put various kinds of rackets in them, but all should have strings. Your appearance on the court, dandied up in spotless white and carrying an armful of impressively encased rackets, makes it look as though you are subsidized by some wide-awake tennis firm, which cannot help but terrify the average opponent.

For one week before the match practice bouncing a ball up off the ground by leaning over and swatting it with the strings of the racket held flat. The good players do this to keep from bending down excessively or scraping the edge of the frame when they pick up a ball. The danger is that sometimes the ball will not come up no matter how hard you swat it. If this happens, stare at the strings, go to the sidelines, extract a new racket, and go after the ball again. Use a Western grip and remember to *concentrate*.

The day before the match rub grass on your tennis shoes and on three fairly new tennis balls. On greeting your opponent you inform him that the day before you just got through playing the final at Southampton, or some such high-class place, and the greenish balls have been used only for the official seven games so they will do for the warm-up. Then, producing an empty bottle of white shoe polish from your bag, you mention that you have run out of the stuff—which is very good for masking the green on your shoes—and ask if you can borrow some of his. He will not have any and you can raise your eyebrows slightly—like a courteous reaction to a person who says he has never seen an automobile.

Before stepping onto the court, you spin very formally for service with one of your rackets. If you win the toss, look around as though examining the light and breeze, then stare as your opponent and with a mysterious smile tell him you'll receive. Already he thinks he has lost two games—the one where you powder his service all over the court and the one where he is aced four straight times. If he wins the toss, he will probably elect to serve.

You give a slight nod of approval, as if to say, "That's exactly the choice Rod Laver would have made," and stroll to the net. You measure this with great exactitude, fiddling with the strap if necessary. Getting your opponent to crank the net up or down while you supervise from the center is worth at least three games to you. He may go into a fit of temper trying to lower it or raise it to your exact specifications. Or he may injure his hand when the crank strikes back. We can fly to the moon but we cannot invent a tennis-net crank that will not tear your hand to pieces if you do not treat it like a vial of nitroglycerine.

Now the warm-up. You can prepare him for a possible surprise by saying, as you stroll out, "I hope I can get used to clay (or whatever) after that damned grass circuit." And, "You'll have to excuse my backhand. 'Muscles'—that's what we call Rosewall—is trying to get me to hit down the line with a touch more underspin." Further protection is afforded by calmly refusing to hit any ball that does not land extremely close to you. This will not only irritate your opponent but lead him to think that you are used to rallying with players so accurate that they can hit the ball in the middle of the court at reasonable depth any time they want to. When retrieving the balls, be very leisurely and pick them up with the racket bounce. During the rally, if you cannot get the ball over the net or keep hitting it out of bounds, change rackets. That is why it is good to have five rackets. If you have only two and keep changing them, your opponent is apt to call over something like, "Why don't you use them both at once, for God's sake?", and you know the spell has been broken.

In keeping with the image of grandeur you are seeking to maintain, you should compliment him when he makes the most ordinary return. For instance, during actual play, if you should send up a short lob that he smashes, say, "Oh, well hit! Beautiful return!", the idea being he had to put forth a superhuman effort to make the shot.

Intimidating Your Opponent

Similarly, when your second serve bounces in the center of the box and he hits it back and you miss it, say, "Nice get! Incredible", as though the serve had nicked the back line with terrific spin and he had to make a desperate lunge for it and was lucky to get his racket on it, let alone make a return.

When he misses a shot, pretend you are in a conspiracy with him to help him make the best showing possible against you. Give him advice (the more puzzling, the better) like, "Your elbow was too loose. Try to tighten it up a little." "Put more weight on the back part of your front foot on the backswing." What you have to do is convince him that, despite the physical evidence, at some point all your skills, dormant since you left Southampton, will return with a rush and you will start using Rosewall's backhand and perhaps Kramer's forehand and blow him off the court. This foreboding about the future cannot help but disconcert him, and he will hit with less assurance lest it wake the sleeping dragon. At worst, you have set the stage for about ten solid alibis to explain why you played the way you did, and this will lessen the anguish of losing.

I have already mentioned how calls and the way calls are made can affect the course and sometimes the outcome of a match. (If I didn't, I certainly meant to.) In tournaments their importance is magnified by about ten. Let me cite a few of my own experiences. In a doubles tournament a few years ago, I was receiving in the first game. The server hit a very hard, flat serve that landed at least three inches out. I saw it, my partner saw it, and the opposing net man saw it. It was out. You could see the mark. But from the server's reaction you would have thought the ball hit eight inches in. "Out?" he screamed, lowering his racket. "You called that *out*?" "It was out," I told him. He stared at me for fifteen seconds as though I had raped his bride a half-hour before the wedding. Finally his net man turned around and said something and he served the second ball. "My God," I thought as I nervously knocked it into the net. "If he raises all that fuss about a ball that far out, how is he going to behave later on if we should happen to call a couple of really *close* ones on him? He will chew the net up."

He was very mild for the rest of the match, however, and my side won in straight sets. I learned later that he reacted the way he did because he had never, in all his years of play, gotten his first serve in, and this particular shot came so close—at a psychologically important time —that he was dismayed that it had not landed in. His partner, who was not too crazy about him, revealed this to me. The incident proves, I think, that you should not let yourself be buffaloed by a case of hysterics on the court. If a shot is out, call it out. Especially when you have two extra witnesses.

In a tournament a year afterward, another partner and I were amazed at the aggressive play of one of our opponents, a little fellow with a chop, named Regis. Regis was always scampering up to net, putting pressure on us, making us miss. Finally, in one desperate rally, my partner hit a weak lob to him, and Regis almost fell down trying to get his racket on the ball. It developed he was not aggressive; he was *suspicious*.

You have probably heard that players like Cliff Richey and Vic Seixes, when they play tournaments, expect about three bad calls per match from the linesmen and hope their opponent will receive an equal number, so the bad calls cancel out, so to speak. But from some unhappy experiences, Regis expected about three bad calls *per game*, and he wanted to be up at net where he would not have to sight through it and he wanted as close a view as possible. As soon as we had correctly surmised that was his purpose—not volleying—we kept hitting to him and won handily.

One time in a singles tournament an opponent made my blood turn to molten metal with this chestnut: With the score 3–all in the third set, I hit a beautiful shot past him at net. He dove for it, missed, and cried "Out" after it hit. From a state of exultation I quickly progressed into one of murderous rage. Adrenalin started bubbling all over my nerve ends. "—of reach," my opponent added with a wry smile.

I glared at him for about twelve seconds, waiting for the various chemicals in my system to become less active. Then I turned and walked to the baseline. "It was in a foot at least," he called, somewhat mockingly. I took about fifteen deep breaths before serving. For the rest of the match I tried to lure him forward with a drop shot and take his head off with a drive, but my coordination had vanished with my equanimity and I blew three games and the match.

Another time I was playing in a doubles tournament against the same judge I mentioned earlier. He hit a short lob that I let bounce, and, since his partner the lawyer was at net (and not too quick), I hit a terrific down-the-line smash that whooshed past his racket on the forehand side. It landed, I was sure, at least two feet in.

"Too bad!" cried the judge, sauntering after the ball.

Again my mood changed from euphoria to murder. "You mean to tell me that shot was *out?*" I yelled.

"Oh, no. It was three feet in," he called cheerily.

"Then what the hell did you say 'Too bad' for?" I shouted.

"I meant it was too bad that George missed it," he said, returning the ball.

Pancho Segura could not have gotten back that shot, I thought. The lawyer missed it—I don't think he even saw it—by a foot. My partner stood around in his usual comatose state, dangling his racket. "What's the score?" he wanted to know. It took me four games to gather some control of my nerves, and we were lucky to win the set.

If such calls, fraught with misunderstanding, can upset an experienced player like myself, you can imagine how they affect the average player under tournament-match pressures.

As far as calling shots is concerned in tournament play, my advice is to establish credibility very early in the match. This is done by calling even questionable shots by your opponent good, and when they are bad, expressing regret—"I'm sorry but I'm afraid I'll have to call that a little bit long" and "Oh! You just went over the line!" It is a mistake to say on a shot that lands good, "You'd kill me if I called that one out." This kind of reaction will set the wheels of his mind to turning. He should be made to think that you are a flawless automaton in announcing the calls and utterly reliable. You can add to the illusion by calling some of your own shots out —when they land a few feet beyond the line; and, when they land a few feet in, questioning his call of "Good!" in a sportsmanlike way, managing to gracefully lose the argument. He will begin to think you are a paragon of honesty, and when the close calls come up later on—as they surely must—you can make a few withdrawals from your integrity bank, as it were, which may be quite useful.

The questions sometimes arise: What are the important games to win? What are the important points to win? You are probably aware that in doubles it is important to win the first point because if you then win the second you put a great deal of pressure on your opponents. If you win the third there is even more pressure. In singles it is a good idea to build up as big a lead as possible on your opponent's serve because these are the games you are going to have to win to stay in the match.

As far as critical games in a set are concerned, it was Tilden's theory that you should try very hard to win the fifth, seventh, and ninth games of a set. This is because if the score is, say, 4–2, the player with four games almost has a lock on the set if he wins the next one; while his opponent manages to remain in the battle if *he* should win it, bringing the score to 4–3. For this reason, or similar ones, it is probably also advisable (my theory) to win the fourth, sixth, and eighth games, if possible. Certainly the more games you win, the better your chances are of taking the set. Strategic thinking like this will become second nature to you after a few tournaments.

10

Courtesy Today

Probably no game in the world is so imbued with a consciousness of correct behavior and courtesy as tennis. Crowds are supposed to remain silent during the play of a point, the calls of linesmen are not to be challenged, and if your opponent almost removes your gallbladder with a smash you are supposed to congratulate him on his fine shot. Temperamental outbursts are frowned on, and you even find some players apologizing when their opponent gets a bad bounce or tosses the ball up crooked on his serve.

Most of the rules of courtesy are known to players of any experience, but there are a few special cases (particularly with the immense growth of indoor tennis) where new rules of courtesy have had to be drawn up or, from the standpoint of practicality, have had to be reinterpreted. Here they are:

Serving

If your net man prudently plays fairly far back when you serve, do not, in your zeal to foot-fault, come any

Tennis on a Rich Man's Court

closer to the net than he is before hitting the ball.

Do not bounce the ball more than twelve times before serving, especially if you are unable to catch it consistently.

When you are playing "first serve in" at the beginning of a match, do not serve more than twenty times in the hope of hitting an ace. Not that an ace is not useful, but you will exhaust yourself for the next four games.

Receiving

The cry of "Take two!" or "Take another!" is a welcome sound for the server to hear after he has served a fault. There are times when it is proper for the receiving team to grant him this extra serve and times when it is not. The server is *not* entitled to an extra serve when:

His own net man encourages him to take it.

A friendly spectator offers it to him.

He fails to catch the ball while bouncing it before serving and has to chase it back to the fence.

Through his own avoirdupois he cannot extract the second ball from his pocket and gets all flustered and tense and finally rips his pants.

The server *is* entitled to an extra serve, however, if:

(Indoors) The lights go out and do not come on again for twenty minutes after he has served the first ball.

An Act of God occurs, like a runaway bulldozer smashing through the wall while he is making the toss for his first serve.

(Outdoors) Your return of an out serve goes over the fence behind him, and he has to quickly rescue the ball from going down a sewer.

(Indoors or out) You, as receiver, call the serve out before it lands, then return it, saying it was good, and, after your partner misses the opponent's return, develop second thoughts about the serve, finally deciding it was out.

You were not ready, and your return goes into the net.

The first serve to you was an ace but your partner is not sure if the ball was in or out.

Mixed Doubles

It is courtesy to let your lady partner serve first unless you are interested in winning.

If the lady on the opposite side calls a shot out that was manifestly in, do not argue but give your own lady partner a long look with one eyebrow raised higher than the other.

Do not hit smashes at the lady player on the other side unless she starts it.

If you are playing mixed doubles on your honeymoon, let your wife serve first.

When Playing on a Rich Man's Private Court

If the host is your partner, let him serve first.

If you are playing against him, do not hit any slices or cuts to him, or drop shots.

Do not serve to his backhand.

If he wants to talk business or politics before playing, do not act impatient but keep nodding.

Be very polite and affable to his sister-in-law if she should happen to be watching.

Do not complain about the bounce, leaves on the court, crooked lines, or thorns growing through the back fence that cut you to pieces when you have to retrieve a ball.

Do not make wisecracks to your host like, "That's a nice sweater you have on. Are you going skiing afterward?"

Do not offer him any tactical advice whatsoever. But if he asks you what is wrong with his grip, show him how you hold the racket, after which you will probably miss four straight points.

Admire his police dog when he gambols all over the court during a critical rally. Do not hit it in the nose with your racket, for several reasons.

Profanity

In the days of bustles and long flannel pants on the court, players were extremely circumspect in their behavior and language. Words of a pejorative nature were not even thought of, let alone voiced. With changing times, however, increased pressures, the existence of a stronger competitive urge among athletes, and greater freedom permitted in almost every area of endeavor, a certain amount of mild pejorative comment is, under certain circumstances, acceptable before and during play. It is permissible to use strong language on the court if:

A beautiful lob that would have caught the opponents flat-footed on a vital point hits the girders, purlins, or light fixtures a few feet overhead, losing you the point merely because the owner wanted to save money.*

The lights go out on all the courts halfway through a set and stay off for five or ten minutes, allowing you the privilege of telling ghost stories at $16 per hour.

* The subject of profanity reminds me that I used to play doubles with a gentleman who invariably missed his first serve and, just as he hit his weak and shallow second serve, would shout out a word of terrifying pejorative strength—his means of letting the other players and any spectators know that he usually hit a harder, deeper second serve (though he never did). This was indoors, where the words bounce off the walls. One time I got into a mixed doubles match with him and wondered if he would keep his mouth shut when he served the second ball or risk shocking the lady players five or six times during the game. He solved the problem by uttering some New Testament words that the ladies had probably never heard before but that would have shocked a gentleman of the cloth had he been present. I would like to see him play mixed doubles with a cleric as his male opponent. He would have to get his first serve in.

Your wife has forgotten to pack your sneakers in your satchel, and you are already ten minutes late for an indoor session with three very nervous players.

The pro on the next court has a lady pupil who keeps banging balls over the separating net into your court during rallies and he thinks it is mighty amusing.

Through a peculiar combination of humidity, temperature, and atmospheric pressure, it is raining harder inside the building than outside, and one of the three balls you are playing with lands in a small lake at one corner of the court.

You learn that the missing ball for which you have been hunting for five minutes under bushes, behind rollers, and on nearby courts has been safely ensconced in the pants pocket of one of your opponents all the time.

General

Throwing Points. Once in a while (a very great while, I would say) it is incumbent on a player to purposely throw a point. If an umpire or linesman makes an extremely bad call against your opponent that the entire audience is aware of, or if, in another case, your opponent blows an easy placement because a bee frightened him while he was lining up the shot (but he refused to play the point over), you may feel you want to chivalrously even things up by giving him the next point. Do not be oversubtle about it—or ironheads in the audience will think you merely choked, and so will your opponent. If you are serving in this situation, make a spectacular double-fault—hit one ball over the fence behind your opponent and the second at the umpire's chair. If you are receiving, drop your racket on the court as your opponent serves and catch the ball, stare at it for a second, toss it back, and call, "Your point, old fellow." There is no advantage in making a noble gesture if it is

The Winner's Leap

going to go unappreciated. Of course, if it is a vital point —like game point—forget all about chivalry.

The Carry. If your opponents accuse you of making a carry, do not deny it but disavow any knowledge of what a carry is. Have them explain and demonstrate at length and *then* deny it. Meanwhile your partner is getting his wind back.

Leaping over the Net. In the highest tennis circles it is customary for the winner of a match to leap over the net with great élan and exuberance to congratulate the loser on his fine play and sportsmanship, even if the score was 6–0, 6–0, 6–0. (At least he did not strike any of the ballboys.) Should you follow this tradition? I strongly advise against it. You may mistime your leap, fail to reach the proper height, and stumble in midair over the net, plummeting to earth and breaking an elbow—and the ignominy and the sight of your opponent laughing are as bad as the pain. Secondly, you may have the score wrong. I remember a few years ago I won a match—so I thought—6–2, 3–6, 8–6, and after the last point I used my remaining measure of strength to jump the net and gleefully seized my opponent's hand and shook it. He backed away and looked perplexed. Then he said, "What the hell are you doing over here? It's *deuce*." Thinking back, I realized he was right. So I returned to my side of the court by the netpost route, while the crowd buzzed, and promptly lost the game and the match. Since then I have told a few players who have leapt over the net after defeating me that they have made a mistake about the score. Actually they haven't, but it is interesting to see the expression on their faces. And at least it cures them of leaping over the net.

If you remember to follow these rules of courtesy on the court you will find the game of tennis much more enjoyable.